Individual
Rights and Civic
Responsibility

THE RIGHT
TO FREE SPEECH

Claudia Isler

The Rosen Publishing Group, Inc.

*For Eric, as always, and in memory of Marvin Mazur, to whom
I always spoke freely*

Published in 2001 by The Rosen Publishing Group, Inc.
29 East 21st Street, New York, NY 10010

First Edition

Library of Congress Cataloging-in-Publication Data

Isler, Claudia.
The right to free speech / by Claudia Isler.— 1st ed.
p. cm. — (Individual rights and civic responsibility)
Includes bibliographical references and index.
ISBN 0-8239-3234-6 (library binding)
1. Freedom of speech—United States—Juvenile literature.
[1. Freedom of speech.] I. Title. II. Series.
KF4772.Z9 I83 2001
342.73'0853—dc21

        2001002097

Manufactured in the United States of America

Contents

Introduction

You may frequently hear people claim, "It's a free country. I can say what I want." Have you ever thought about what those words really mean? In which ways are you free to speak and act as you please? When is it not only reasonable but also necessary for a society to set limits on individual and/or group expression?

For example, imagine you are sitting in the park, talking with your friends, and you say, "You know, the 2000 presidential election was fixed. There must have been a conspiracy. That's the only way George W. Bush won." The person sitting on the next bench overhears you. She voted for Bush, and she becomes suspicious of you. She finds a police officer and points to you, saying, "She spoke against the president and questioned the integrity of the American electoral process. She is a threat to this society. Arrest her for treason!" In the United States people found guilty of treason have been accused of spying for other countries. What if the police officer arrested you and sent you to jail?

Let's say you win an award from the city council for volunteer work, and you have to give an acceptance speech. You do a lot of research, quoting a number of people who have inspired you. You also mention your god, because you believe that your religion provides you with strength and devotion to caring for others. A few days before the awards ceremony, you must submit your speech for the board's approval. The board tells you that the speech is fine, but that you must take out any mention of your god, as it might offend some members of the community. Do you know whether the First Amendment protects your right to talk about your religious beliefs?

Pretend that you work for a real-estate business that rents out apartments in your city. While filing rental applications, you notice a pattern. It seems that codes on the applications indicate the renters' race or ethnicity, and the real-estate agency has repeatedly turned down applications from members of certain groups. You decide that the way to force the business to adopt equal opportunity practices is to call the local television news station for media coverage and arrange to picket outside the office. Do you know whether the First Amendment protects your right to bring attention to the agency's practices?

The First Amendment

Freedom of speech is a right protected by the First Amendment to the Constitution. The Constitution was written in 1787. It describes the principles that govern America. The Bill of Rights, the first ten amendments to the Constitution, was added in 1791 to guarantee individual liberties. Each state also wrote its own constitution, and

More than two centuries after the Bill of Rights was added to the Constitution, what the First Amendment right to free speech guarantees remains a contentious issue.

most of these contained a bill of rights that guaranteed freedom of expression. At the same time, the framers of the Constitution realized that there might need to be limits placed upon what people could say. But they debated the question of what these limits would be.

The Constitution is short, and its language is general, in part to address this problem. It has been able to adapt to changing times. The framers of the Constitution wanted to protect American citizens from the injustices they had suffered while living under English common law and the rule of King George. The men who wrote the Constitution and the Bill of Rights were also deeply affected by an intellectual current known as the Enlightenment.

The Enlightenment

In the middle of the eighteenth century, some European thinkers began to analyze nature in search of universal

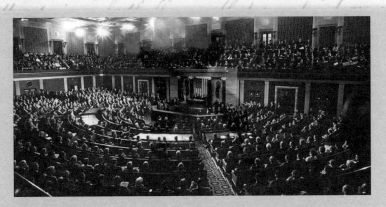

The First Amendment

Congress shall make no law respecting an establishment of religion, or prohibiting the free exercise thereof; or abridging the freedom of speech, or of the press; or the right of the people peaceably to assemble, and to petition the Government for a redress of grievances.

laws that governed the world. They believed that the universe was an ordered and orderly creation. Above all, these philosophers emphasized acquiring knowledge through reason, or rational thought, and challenging previously unquestioned assumptions. This philosophical movement was called the Enlightenment.

Enlightenment rationalism affected primarily the realms of science and politics. Philosopher John Locke's *Two Treatises of Government* and other works by French and Scottish philosophers questioned the legitimacy of hierarchical and monarchical rule. They believed that because people created governments, people should remain free to change them. At the time, they understood the word "people" to mean only propertied white men.

Nevertheless, this was a decidedly radical philosophy in its day. They also contended that a government should serve the good of the people. A ruler who broke his or her contract with the people and who failed to protect their rights could be removed legitimately from power. Interestingly, today we often rely on the justices of the United States Supreme Court, who are appointed by the president rather than elected, to help define our rights under the First Amendment.

The Court System

The United States court system is divided into two separate systems, federal and state. The court system is organized hierarchically, in that higher courts can hear cases previously tried in lower courts, and can either uphold or overturn a lower court's decision.

Federal Court

The federal system is divided into three levels. The first is federal district court, followed by the United States courts of appeals, and then the ultimate judicial authority in the country, the United States Supreme Court. The federal district court system has at least one bench or court in each state as well as one in Washington, DC, and one in Puerto Rico. Each district has from one to twenty judges, who are appointed by the president. Among other things, the district court oversees cases that involve violations of the Constitution or other federal laws.

The U.S. courts of appeals are superior to the district courts. Sometimes called the circuit courts, they consist of eleven judicial circuits throughout the states, with another in Washington, DC. Depending on the circuit, these courts can be staffed with anywhere from six to twenty-seven judges. These courts hear appeals from the district courts and also hear cases that challenge the orders of any federal agency.

Since 1869, the Supreme Court has had one chief justice and eight associate justices. The Supreme Court has the final say on all cases that it hears. The Supreme Court reviews decisions in cases made by the U.S. courts of appeals, or even by state appeals courts, if the case involves a federal or constitutional issue.

State Court

The state system is a lot more complicated than the federal one, and no two states maintain exactly the same system. Like the federal system, the state court system is hierarchical. The lowest level of the state courts, known as the inferior courts, can include municipal court, traffic court, or the justice of the peace. These courts hear only minor civil or criminal cases.

Superior courts, also known as state district courts or circuit courts, hear cases about more serious crimes as well as appeals from inferior courts. Decisions in these courts are decided by jury. The highest state courts go by a variety of names: state supreme court, the appellate court, or state court of appeals. They hear appeals from the state superior courts and occasionally has original jurisdiction over very important cases. In between these three levels are a variety of other courts. The number of these courts varies from state to state.

Why Freedom of Speech Is Important

Since the creation of the Constitution, people have constantly disputed and attempted to define what types of speech are protected by the First Amendment. Often these disputes arise because Americans continue to transform their society and

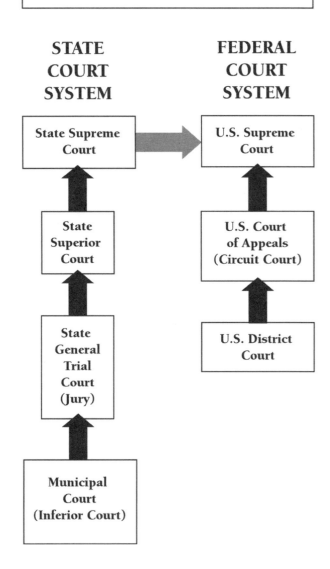

U. S. Court System

STATE COURT SYSTEM

FEDERAL COURT SYSTEM

State Supreme Court → U.S. Supreme Court

State Superior Court

U.S. Court of Appeals (Circuit Court)

State General Trial Court (Jury)

U.S. District Court

Municipal Court (Inferior Court)

The American court system is a hierarchy of state and federal courts, with the United States Supreme Court being the ultimate judicial authority on the constitutionality of American laws.

give voice to their political opinions. For instance, in the nineteenth century and early twentieth century, suffragists Elizabeth Cady Stanton and Susan B. Anthony publicly demanded that American women obtain the right to vote. Similarly, the right to free speech enabled African American civil rights activists, including Dr. Martin Luther King Jr., to demand their rights as American citizens and to demand an end to racial inequality. Many people in the late 1960s and early 1970s utilized their right to free speech to protest the war in Vietnam. Today, people continue to struggle for the right to be heard. People also continue to fight for the right to read, say, listen to, watch, and think about whatever they choose.

When we talk about freedom of speech, we usually focus on freedom rather than speech. Speech is an ambiguous concept. Every day, as new technologies unfold and become basic parts of our communications, what we mean by "speech" expands. The resulting reaction to different forms of speech (on television, in movies, and over the Internet) is often based on the way speech is communicated and the market or the audience rather than on the strength of the ideas communicated.

New media beg the question: Is any word, image, or act that has meaning considered speech? It is difficult to say, and, in fact, begs another question: Is speech limited to the idea being communicated, or does it include the mode of communication, or both? In other words, can the First Amendment be used to regulate what you see on the Internet, on television, and in the newspaper? While some modes of communication are new, the struggle to define the concept of speech and to interpret the right to free speech has a long and complex history.

1 Interpreting Speech

People who study and write about the First Amendment have varying interpretations as to when and why speech warrants protection. Some constitutional experts interpret the right narrowly, arguing that the free speech clause of the First Amendment only protects the spoken word. Others believe in a broader understanding of the First Amendment, claiming that it also protects actions that express an opinion, or speech acts. These advocates claim that the First Amendment protects freedom of expression and not simply freedom of speech.

Among more recent speech-act controversies is flag burning. Historically, people have burned the flag to protest government policies. To others, the flag is a sacred object that should never be burned. These people argue that burning a flag is an act, and not a form of speech, and should therefore not be protected by the First Amendment. The Supreme Court has ruled that flag burning is symbolic speech. In 1989, the Supreme Court ruled in *Texas v. Johnson* that this symbolic speech is protected under the First Amendment.

Other types of free-speech acts can include protest marches or sit-ins. The problem, some say, with considering certain actions "free speech," lies in the regulation of those actions. As scholar Stanley Fish notes in Franklyn S. Haiman's *Speech Acts and the First Amendment,* "No one would think to frame a First Amendment that began 'Congress shall make no law abridging freedom of action'; for that would amount to saying 'Congress shall make no law,' which would amount to saying 'There shall be no law.'" Regulating what people do is a tricky business, and Americans contradict themselves all the time when they argue about the First Amendment and the right to free speech. One Supreme Court case in particular examined the distinction between a free-speech act and disorderly conduct.

Feiner v. New York (1951)

Irving Feiner, a college student in Syracuse, New York, was arrested on March 3, 1949, for breaking New York's disorderly conduct law. The law states:

> Any person who, with intent to provoke a breach of the peace: (1) uses offensive, disorderly, threatening, abusive, or insulting language, conduct, or behavior; (2) acts in such a manner as to annoy, disturb, interfere with, obstruct, or be offensive to others; or (3) congregates with others on a public street and refuses to move on when ordered by the police; shall be deemed to have committed the offense of disorderly conduct.

Before his arrest, Feiner had stood on a box to address a racially diverse crowd of almost seventy-five people. The police who were called to the scene to investigate heard Feiner say, "The Negroes don't have equal rights; they should rise up in arms and fight for their rights," and "President Truman is a bum." The crowd began to react, some in favor of Feiner's ideas and some against them. There was some pushing and shoving. The police ordered Feiner to stop speaking, because they thought he would start a riot. Feiner was arrested when he refused to end his speech. He was tried and convicted in the Syracuse City Court.

Feiner appealed his conviction in both the county and state courts of appeals, both of which upheld the city's verdict. He appealed to the U.S. Supreme Court, arguing that his right to free speech had been violated under the Fourteenth Amendment. The Fourteenth Amendment protects the individual rights outlined in the Bill of Rights by prohibiting individual states from denying those rights. If a state passes a law that limits free speech, the Fourteenth Amendment protects citizens from having to obey such a law.

The Supreme Court did not see it Feiner's way. He had been asked to come down off his box three times before he was arrested. The court believed that he had not been arrested for what he had said. The crowd that had gathered while Feiner was speaking became angry, with one onlooker threatening violence if the police did not take action to stop Feiner. In addition, pedestrians were forced to walk in a street that was open to traffic to avoid the crowd on the sidewalk. Chief Justice Fred Vinson delivered the verdict: " . . . the imminence of greater disorder coupled with [Feiner's] deliberate defiance of the police officers convinced us that we should not reverse this conviction in the name of free speech." Feiner had not been arrested for suggesting that African Americans ought to fight for their rights, nor for criticizing the president. He was arrested because he did not move when told to do so by the police, as the disorderly conduct law stipulates. He was arrested also for disturbing the peace because arguments were breaking out in the crowd that had gathered to hear him.

Limiting Speech

Today, some Americans believe in strict limitations on free speech and speech acts. The January 8, 2000 edition of the *Washington Post National Weekly Edition* reported the results of a survey of 1,015 randomly selected adults. Thirty-one percent of the respondents said that they would not allow a rally in their community for a cause that might offend some community members. Two out of three would not allow people to say things in public that might offend racial groups. And 53 percent would make it illegal to make racist remarks in public. Furthermore, according to the *Post* article, the people surveyed who said they would support laws against offensive speech also said they would support government action to "enforce their preferences." Also, more than half of the people surveyed said they would support a federal ratings system for Internet content.

Protecting Speech

While the *Post* survey indicates that some Americans support great restrictions on speech, many Americans consider protecting free speech integral to preserving democracy in the

United States. Americans can exercise their freedom of speech to some degree in some, but not all, public spaces. You may exercise your right to free speech in public places, such as parks and streets. Such places are called public forums. Not all public spaces qualify, however. For instance, you may not begin political rallies in the post office or in the welfare office. The government may also regulate the time at which demonstrations occur and the way in which citizens use public space.

The American Civil Liberties Union

The American Civil Liberties Union (ACLU) is a nonpartisan organization that was established in 1920. Its goal is to protect the rights guaranteed to Americans by the Constitution. It focuses on freedom of expression and equality before the law. The ACLU has a very large membership; it has been involved in nearly every important civil liberties case since its inception. According to the ACLU, the First Amendment protects speech, no matter how offensive it is. In a summary of their goals and policies, the ACLU states, "How much we value the right of free speech is put to its severest test when the speaker is someone we disagree with most."

The Right to Know

Some lawmakers felt that the right to know information, especially information contained in government records, was an integral part of the right to free speech. Consequently, the Freedom of Information Act was passed in 1966. As a result, all noncriminal issues filed with the courts are considered public records. For example, if you are thinking of buying a house and want to know if the

Members of the Supreme Court in 1991, from left to right: *(top)* David H. Souter, Antonin Scalia, Anthony M. Kennedy, Clarence Thomas; *(bottom)* John Paul Stevens, Byron R. White, Chief Justice William H. Rehnquist, Harry A. Blackmun, and Sandra Day O'Connor

asking price is fair, you can look up how much the present owners paid for it when they bought it.

Some information is not public. For instance, we do not have free access to adoption records. This is to protect both the adopted child and the biological parents. The Supreme Court ruled on the right to information in the 1991 case *Rust v. Sullivan*. The court decided that the U.S. Department of Health and Human Services could prevent health care providers (who receive federal funds) from informing women about abortion or abortion providers.

Obviously, the American court system continues to struggle to define speech. Americans utilize their right to free speech to change their lives and their communities. As they do so, conflict may ensue. Certainly, many disputes regarding free speech in the past have found their way to the courts. Actually, the seeds of the struggle were planted when America was no more than thirteen colonies of the British Empire.

2 History of the First Amendment

The Constitution of the United States and its first ten amendments, the Bill of Rights, were written by many of the same people who led the American Revolution (1775–1783). In 1776, the Continental Congress appointed a committee to write what would become known as the Declaration of Independence. It was written by Thomas Jefferson and was called "The Unanimous Declaration of the 13 United States of America."

The Congress understood that the document was not simply a statement of withdrawal from the British Empire; it was also about creating a guiding set of principles for governing. To that end, the Declaration speaks of the "inalienable rights" of men, stating "to secure these rights, governments are instituted among men, deriving their just powers from the consent of the governed." In other words, the government obtains its power from the people who choose it; it is not all-powerful in and of itself. Among the inalienable rights the authors believed in were the right to free speech, the right to protest against the government, and the right to object to its policies.

Thomas Jefferson (1743–1826)

Born in Virginia, Jefferson became the third president of the United States, serving two terms. He was also the principal author of the Declaration of Independence. He was vocal in support of the growing opposition in Virginia to the British Parliament's taxation policies and its general control over the American colonies. In his work *A Summary View of the Rights of British America* (1774), Jefferson argued that America's ties to Great Britain were voluntary. In 1784, Jefferson succeeded Benjamin Franklin as American minister to France. He served two consecutive terms as president of the United States (1801–1809). In later years, Jefferson referred to his election as president as the "Revolution of 1800." Jefferson was delighted that his victory ended Federalist control of the national government. Jefferson felt that his victory represented a return to the republican principles of the revolution. One of the greatest accomplishments of his presidency was the Louisiana Purchase, which doubled the area of the United States and opened the trans-Mississippi West for American settlement. He also established the University of Virginia. Although politically opposed to the concept of slavery, during his lifetime Jefferson owned a probable total of 600 slaves and lived a lifestyle that depended upon the institution of slavery.

In the same year, *Common Sense* was published. Its author, Thomas Paine, was a British citizen who moved to America in 1774. A political theorist and a writer, Paine produced a series of sixteen pamphlets during the American Revolution called *The Crisis,* of which *Common Sense* was one. *Common Sense* called for the American colonists to rebel against the British and to declare their independence from the crown. This document helped convince the majority of colonists that revolution was the only solution to their disenchantment with British rule. Paine had exercised his inalienable right to express his ideas to the public, even if those ideas criticized or suggested the overthrow of the government.

After the Revolution

A document called the Articles of Confederation maintained order among the association of states during the Revolutionary War, but as the federation of colonies steered toward becoming a young nation, its weaknesses soon became evident. As a result, in mid-May 1787, fifty-five men representing all the states except Rhode Island met in Philadelphia to devise a document that set forth the principles that would guide the newly independent nation's government. It also outlined the form the national government would take. They called this document the Constitution. Specifically, the Constitution provided for more national (as opposed to state) authority, especially over taxation, trade, and foreign commerce.

Those supporting the proposed Constitution called themselves Federalists. They envisioned a strong central government led by aristocratic and talented men. They claimed that the states did not need to fear centralized authority as long as good people were in charge. Unfortunately, as products of the times in which they lived, these men lacked a more inclusive understanding of who was fit to lead. Their understanding of "good people" was limited to propertied, formally educated, white, Christian men like themselves.

The experiences of fighting a war and of struggling for survival as an independent nation changed the political outlook of many Americans in the 1780s. At the outset of the war, most Americans believed that "that government which governs best, governs least." By the late 1780s however, many people had changed their minds. They were the drafters and supporters of the Constitution. Federalists argued that the separation of powers among the legislative, executive, and judicial branches along with the division of state and national powers would ensure that no one group would control the government.

Contrastingly, Antifederalists wanted a weak central government, protection of individual rights, and a loosely regulated economy. The Antifederalists insisted that the Constitution include a bill of rights. The Federalists won the initial battle in that the Constitution was ratified by the states, if only by a narrow margin.

Still, many of the states and Antifederalist members of Congress insisted on adding a bill of rights to the Constitution. Finally, then-Congress member James Madison placed nineteen proposed amendments before the House of Representatives. The states soon ratified ten, which officially became part of the Constitution on December 15, 1791.

The Supreme Court Building in Washington, DC. The words "Equal Justice under Law" are carved above the main entrance.

The Supreme Court

Aside from constitutional amendments, the most far-reaching piece of legislation enacted by the first Congress was the Judiciary Act of 1789. This act defined the jurisdiction of the federal courts and established a six-member Supreme Court, thirteen district courts, and three circuit courts of appeal.

Patrick Henry (1736–1799)

Born in Virginia, Henry studied law after failing at business and farming. He was a delegate to the first and second Continental Congresses. He is remembered for a speech that included the famous line: "I do not know what course others may take, but as for me, give me liberty or give me death." He also served as governor of Virginia. He opposed the new Constitution, arguing that it compromised people's rights. For this reason, he strongly supported and was influential in the creation of the Bill of Rights.

Currently, nine justices, or judges, sit on the Court. The president selects Supreme Court candidates who are then approved by Congress. Because of this power, the Supreme Court has shaped greatly the history of the United States.

Alien and Sedition Acts

A major piece of legislation passed by the Congress of the relatively young nation of the United States of America was a set of laws known as the Alien and Sedition Acts. In 1798, the Federalist-controlled Congress adopted these laws in an effort to suppress dissent. The Alien Acts affected foreign-born residents, or aliens, and provided for the detention of aliens from enemy countries in time of war. Further, it gave the president authority to deport anyone living in the country as an alien who seemed to threaten the nation. The fourth statute, the Sedition Act, sought to control both citizens and aliens. Generally, the act targeted sedition or resistance to government authority. Specifically, it outlawed conspiracies to prevent the enforcement of federal laws, setting the maximum punishment for such offenses at five years in prison and a $5,000 fine.

The Sedition Act also tried to control speech. Writing, printing, or uttering "false, scandalous, and malicious" statements against the government or the president, "with the intent to defame . . . or to bring them or either of them, into contempt or disrepute" became a crime punishable by as much as two years imprisonment and a fine of $2,000. Today, any such law punishing speech alone would be considered unconstitutional. But in the eighteenth century, when a fledgling nation struggled to establish federal order, organized political opposition became highly suspect. As a result, many Americans supported the Sedition Act's restriction on speech.

In response to these severe measures, in 1798 and 1799, the Kentucky and Virginia state legislatures passed resolutions contradicting the Alien and Sedition Acts. In fact, the Kentucky resolution stated that the government had no right to exercise powers not granted by the Constitution, and a state could undo federal laws if they were unfair. In the early years of the nineteenth century, these acts that unfairly targeted recently arrived immigrants expired or were repealed. Nevertheless, regulating sedition and the corresponding effects that such attempts have on the right to free speech remained hotly debated issues throughout American history.

3 **Sedition**

World War I broke out more than 100 years after the framers of the Constitution had guaranteed the right to free speech. The Great War, as it was known, lasted from 1914 to 1918. As the nation was at war, this era revived questions of speech, protest, and sedition. Many wondered: Do Americans have the right to voice their disagreement with government policy, especially during times of national crisis?

The war was fought in Europe between the Allies (France, Great Britain, Russia, and the United States) and the Central Powers (Germany, Austria-Hungary, and Turkey). It was one of the bloodiest wars in history: 65 million men and women served in the military, and about 10 million people were killed. Twice that number were wounded. Naturally, these numbers upset many Americans and fueled antiwar sentiment in the United States.

Initially, President Woodrow Wilson had promised to keep the United States out of the war. In 1915, however, German U-boats assaulted the British passenger ship, *Lusitania*; 128

The United States entered World War I after the German submarine U-139 (bottom) sunk the British liner *Lusitania* (top), killing 128 Americans.

Americans were killed. As American lives had been lost, President Wilson found it impossible to remain neutral. In April 1916, Wilson asked Congress for a declaration of war. America's first congresswoman, Jeannette Rankin, opposed this move. America was divided not only between people against the United States' participation in the war and those for it, but also along ethnic lines. One of every three Americans was either foreign-born or the child of a foreign-born parent. Many of the 32 million Americans with strong family ties to foreign

Jeannette Rankin (1880–1973)

Rankin was a suffragist and a pacifist. She was also the first woman elected to Congress, serving two terms, one beginning in 1917, and the other in 1941. In 1917, just four days after she took her seat in Congress, she was one of the representatives who voted against declaring war on Germany, saying, "I want to stand by my country, but I cannot vote for war." She also voted against the Espionage Act of 1917. In the 1920s, she was an officer of the Women's International League for Peace and Freedom, and she served as a lobbyist for the Women's Peace Union, where she campaigned to outlaw war. In 1929, she joined the National Council for the Prevention of War. In 1941, she cast the only vote against the declaration of war on Japan, and in 1968, she led a group of about 5,000 people to Washington, DC, where they demonstrated against the Vietnam War.

nations came from countries that were considered enemies, such as Germany and Austria-Hungary. Wilson believed he needed to develop a way to unify the American people against the European enemies. One method President Wilson devised was the Committee on Public Information (CPI).

The Committee on Public Information

Formed in 1917, the Committee on Public Information endeavored to convince the American public to support the war effort enthusiastically. Simply put, the CPI wanted to sell the war. To that end, the CPI implemented an enormous propaganda campaign. Propaganda is information, often incomplete or prejudiced, that is spread to influence the way people think.

CPI hired approximately 75,000 speakers, known as "four-minute men," who gave moving, patriotic speeches in schools, churches, movie theaters, and other public places. It distributed millions of pamphlets in a number of languages explaining America's role in the war. It even produced CPI movies, including *Kaiser: The Beast of Berlin*. Kaiser was the official title of the ruler of Germany. Another film, *To Hell with the Kaiser*, was so popular that Massachusetts riot police were called in to calm an angry mob that had been turned away at an overcrowded theater.

The committee also engaged in censorship (the cutting out) of allegedly dangerous information. Journalists were given official guidelines about what they could say and write. Businesses were encouraged to spy on their employees. The CPI urged neighbors to spy on neighbors and to report any supposedly disloyal feelings they sensed or observed. Not surprisingly, an atmosphere of deep mistrust enveloped the entire country.

The Espionage Act of 1917 and the Sedition Act of 1918

The American government became obsessed with silencing dissenting political opinion. Congress passed the Espionage Act in 1917, which was amended by the Sedition Act in 1918.

The Sedition Act, 1918

Section three of the act states:

Whoever, when the United States is at war, shall willfully make or convey false reports or false statements with intent to interfere with the operation or success of the military or naval forces of the United States, or to promote the success of its enemies, or shall willfully make or convey false reports, or false statements . . . or incite insubordination [disobedience], disloyalty, mutiny [rebellion], or refusal of duty, in the military or naval forces of the United States, or shall willfully obstruct . . . the recruiting or enlistment service of the United States, or . . . shall willfully utter, print, write, or publish any disloyal, profane, scurrilous, or abusive language about the form of government of the United States . . . or shall willfully display the flag of any foreign enemy, or shall willfully . . . urge, incite, or advocate any curtailment [reduction] of production . . . or advocate, teach, defend, or suggest the doing of any of the acts or things in this section enumerated [listed] and whoever shall by word or act oppose the cause of the United States therein, shall be punished by a fine of not more than $10,000 or imprisonment for not more than twenty years, or both . . .

The amendment made it illegal to criticize the war or the government in any way. German Americans could not voice worries about their homeland or relatives, nor could any American citizen say, out loud in public, "We should not be at war." Playing German music and teaching or speaking the German language were prohibited. In everyday conversation, familiar German words were replaced, so that "sauerkraut" became "liberty cabbage" or "victory cabbage." Songs such as "Oh, Tannenbaum" (Oh, Christmas Tree) were ripped from books of Christmas carols. Towns changed German street names. People who were seen as pro-German were pressured to change their German-sounding names, were chased out of their jobs, and in a few cases, were beaten or murdered. The country had been overtaken with the very same intense nationalism that had ignited World War I. Eventually, the act came under fire—it seemed unconstitutional, but the Supreme Court had the final say.

Schenck v. United States (1919)

Charles Schenck was the general secretary of the United States Socialist Party. The party's main office was in Philadelphia. The party campaigned against the war and against drafting people to fight it. In 1917, under Schenck's direction, the group hoped to send out letters to 15,000 draft-age men. The letters argued that conscription, or the draft, was despotic and urged the men to resist the call to arms. "If you do not assert and support your rights, you are helping to deny or disparage rights which it is the solemn duty of all citizens and residents of the United States to retain." The letters concluded, "You must do your share to maintain, support, and uphold the rights of the people of this country."

The police raided the party's headquarters, took all the mailings, and arrested Schenck. He was accused of violating the Espionage Act by passing out antiwar literature. In federal district court, he was tried for conspiracy to violate the Espionage Act. Schenck argued that his First Amendment right of free speech rendered the Espionage Act unconstitutional. Nevertheless, Schenck was convicted. He appealed his conviction to the U.S. Supreme Court. Justice Oliver Wendell Holmes explained the decision of the Court:

During World War I, the U.S. Army used posters of Uncle Sam to encourage young men to join the armed forces.

...the character of every act depends upon the circumstances in which it is done. The most stringent protection of free speech would not protect a man in falsely shouting 'fire' in a theater, and causing a panic . . . The question in every case is whether the words used are used in such circumstances and are of such a nature as to create a clear and present danger that they will bring about substantive [material] evils that Congress has a right to prevent . . . When a nation is at war many things that might be said in time of peace are such a hindrance [obstacle] to its effort that their utterance will not be endured so long as men fight, and that no court could regard them as protected by any constitutional right.

The Supreme Court had concluded unanimously that war was a special circumstance in which Americans could not say whatever they liked about the government.

Gitlow v. People (1925)

A somewhat similar case came about as a result of New York State's Criminal Anarchy Law. Passed in 1902, the law stated that it was a crime to try to encourage the violent overthrow of the government. Benjamin Gitlow was a member of the Socialist Party during the 1920s. In 1923, he published and circulated 16,000 copies of the *Left-Wing Manifesto*. The pamphlet supported the creation of a socialist system in the United States through massive strikes and "class action . . . in any form." Gitlow was arrested for circulating these pamphlets and causing political agitation. He was tried and convicted in the New York State Supreme Court, but he appealed to the U.S. Supreme Court, arguing that his First Amendment right to freedom of speech (and of the press) had been violated.

Interestingly, Gitlow had not committed actions that indicated he intended to overthrow the government. The case was only about whether the Constitution protected political agitation through words alone. The court ruled in favor of Gitlow. In its decision, delivered by Justice Oliver Wendell Holmes, the court stated that " . . . for present purposes, we may assume that freedom of speech and of press . . . are among the fundamental personal rights and liberties protected by the due

Jane Addams (1860–1935)

A social worker and pacifist, Addams was dissatisfied with the decorative position women had in society. She wanted to have more of a direct political impact. In one of Chicago's poorest slums, she founded Hull House, a place where young women could help those less fortunate than themselves. It became a center for the neighborhood, a home for girls in need of shelter, a boys' club, a daycare service, and more. It was so popular that settlement houses opened in cities all over the country, and Addams garnered national attention.

Addams was also an officer in the Progressive Party and the Women's International League for Peace and Freedom. Addams and other founding members claimed that women peace advocates had a special role as "the guardians of life." She wrote books on a variety of topics, including *Newer Ideals of Peace*, that explained militarism in the United States. Her objections to war hurt her reputation during World War I; she was called "the most dangerous woman in America" by those influenced by the CPI's propaganda. Eventually, her achievements were recognized again, and she was awarded the Nobel Peace Prize in 1931.

Justice Oliver Wendell Holmes, who wrote the majority opinion in the case of *Gitlow v. People,* argued that the Fourteenth Amendment prohibits states from infringing on the individual's right to free speech.

process clause of the Fourteenth Amendment from impairment by the State." Justice Holmes continued:

> It is said that this manifesto was more than a theory, that it was an incitement. Every idea is an incitement. It offers itself for belief and if believed it is acted on unless some other belief outweighs it or some failure of energy stifles the movement at its birth. The only difference between the expression of an opinion and an incitement in the narrower sense is the speaker's enthusiasm for the result. Eloquence [expressiveness] may set fire to reason. But whatever may be thought of the redundant discourse [speech] before us it had no chance of starting a present conflagration [fire]. If in the long run the beliefs expressed in proletarian dictatorship are destined to be accepted by the dominant forces of the community, the only meaning of free speech is that they should be given their chance and have their way.

As Gitlow's arrest was a violation of free speech by a state rather than by the federal government, Holmes demonstrated that free speech is not specifically protected from state authority in the Constitution. The First Amendment applies only to the federal government. But the "due process of law" clause of the Fourteenth Amendment protects human freedoms generally. Holmes and the majority of the Court recognized this and read into that part of the Fourteenth Amendment, which related to the protections of the First Amendment.

The Right to Free Speech

The Fourteenth Amendment protects our life, liberty, and property, and our right to fair treatment under the law, or due process. Due process means that we will not be unduly punished, and that when we are accused of a crime, we will get a fair trial and a lawyer. The interpretation of due process has changed over time and can refer not only to the procedures those accused undergo, but also to the grounds on which they are accused.

Gitlow was accused on the grounds of trying to violently overthrow the government. The Court realized that the publishing and distribution of pamphlets did not constitute violent overthrow. Consequently, the court concluded that Gitlow's arrest violated his right to free speech, freedom of the press, and his Fourteenth Amendment right to due process.

In arriving at this decision, Justice Holmes recognized a problem we still grapple with today—how do we define the areas protected by the guarantee of free speech? If we do not tolerate others' opinions, how can we save the freedom to speak our own minds? Holmes argued that to preserve freedom generally, the court should preserve the freedom to disagree about matters of importance.

Eugene V. Debs (1855–1926)

Eugene Debs was a political activist who organized the American Railway Union in 1892. He helped to found the Social Democratic Party in 1897, which was renamed the Socialist Party in 1901. He ran for president of the United States in 1900, 1904, 1908, and 1912. In 1912, he won 6 percent of the national vote. In 1918 Debs enthusiastically delivered a speech extolling the virtues of socialism and freedom of speech. He also argued for the right to criticize the Wilson administration for taking America into World War I. Federal agents arrested him. Debs told the court that the Espionage Act was, "a despotic enactment in flagrant conflict with democratic principles and with the spirit of free institutions." Although he received a ten-year sentence, Debs remained in prison until late 1921, when he received a pardon.

4 Protest

Like reformers in the early part of the twentieth century, in the 1960s, many people began to speak out about controversial social and political issues in the United States. The Civil Rights movement consisted of many people who could no longer tolerate segregation and racism in the United States. In response to official and unofficial forms of racial segregation in the United States and to a history of being denied their full rights as American citizens, many African Americans began to organize peaceful protests, marches, and sit-ins.

Boycott

One of the most notable events during the Civil Rights movement was the Montgomery bus boycott. A boycott is a refusal to buy goods or services or to participate in an activity to protest a decision or policy. In December 1955, members of the African American community of Montgomery, Alabama, decided they would no longer ride

Dr. Martin Luther King Jr. (1929–1968)

Born in Atlanta, Georgia, King was a black Baptist minister who led the Civil Rights movement from the mid-1950s until he was assassinated in Memphis, Tennessee, in 1968. His leadership helped the movement fight against segregation. He promoted nonviolent forms of protest, such as sit-ins and marches. He served as the president of the Montgomery Improvement Association, a group of African American activists in Alabama. In his first speech as president, he said: "We have no alternative but to protest. For many years we have shown an amazing patience . . . But we come here tonight to be saved from that patience that makes us patient with anything less than freedom and justice."

From 1960 to 1965, King organized many protest demonstrations, including the March on Washington in 1963. Dr. King was awarded the Nobel Peace Prize in 1964, and he continued his work until his murder. He taught many Americans the value of the right to speak out and the importance of doing so.

city buses until those buses were desegregated. Until that time, African Americans were allowed to sit only in the back of the city buses and were required to give up their seats to white passengers if the bus became crowded. This boycott was a free speech act. It was a physical demonstration of how African Americans felt about segregation.

In 1956, the Supreme Court ruled in *Gayle v. Browder* that segregation on buses was unconstitutional. "We have settled beyond question that no State may require racial segregation of interstate transportation facilities . . . This question is no longer open; it is foreclosed as a litigable issue." By making their voices heard, African Americans had captured an important victory. It took time for governmental authorities to successfully implement the court's ruling, though. Initially, angry whites shot at the buses and their African American passengers, causing the suspension of bus service until the violence stopped.

Sit-Ins

Another form of nonviolent protest is a sit-in: People sit down in a place and refuse to move until a policy is changed. During the Civil Rights movement, one of the first sit-ins took place in Greensboro, North Carolina, in 1960. Four African American college students bought some school supplies in Woolworth's (a nationwide five-and-dime store, now out of business) and then sat down at the store's whites-only lunch counter. They had not been given service by the time the store closed, and so they went home.

Students in the South began to organize more and more sit-ins at whites-only lunch counters. They sat and waited to be served. Waves of student protesters were arrested, only to be replaced at the lunch counter by their fellow protestors. Students in northern states began to picket outside the business chains that refused to serve African Americans in the South. For the most part, the sit-ins were peaceful, but then a group of white teenagers attacked some student protestors in Nashville, Tennessee. Unfortunately, the police only arrested the protesters.

Congress of Racial Equality

In 1942 students at the University of Chicago founded the Congress of Racial Equality, or CORE. For the next twenty years, CORE members trained many civil rights activists about nonviolent means of protest. Until 1955 CORE's membership stemmed from the North and was mostly white. In the 1950s CORE went south, training activists for the Montgomery bus boycott. CORE also gained national attention for participating in lunch-counter sit-ins.

In 1961 CORE appointed its first African American president, James Farmer, who was committed to integration. Voter registration became CORE's new focus, as CORE'S concentration shifted to enhancing African American political power. In 1966, Farmer was replaced by Floyd McKissick, who supported African American separatism. From the time of McKissick's appointment, CORE became an African American organization devoted to political and economic equality for African Americans. CORE also participated in the growing antiwar movement of the Vietnam era, supporting many nonviolent protests and marches.

Sit-ins continued into the following year. Finally, in 1964, the Civil Rights Act was passed. It gave the U.S. attorney general more power to protect American citizens against discrimination and segregation in voting, education, and the use of public facilities.

Cox v. Louisiana (1965)

During the Civil Rights movement, there were countless demonstrations protesting racist policies. In Baton Rouge, Louisiana, twenty-three civil rights protesters, all students at Southern University, were arrested on December 14, 1961. They had been picketing outside stores with segregated lunch counters. On December 15, 2,000 more protesters marched to the Baton Rouge courthouse to demonstrate their objection to these arrests. The chief of police asked them twice to disband as they readied for their march. Reverend B. Elton Cox, field secretary of CORE, led the march.

When the group arrived at the courthouse, Cox was instructed by the chief of police to keep the demonstration on the west side of the street (across the street from the courthouse), which he did. There was a small crowd, mostly of curious courthouse personnel, gathered on the east side of the street, and there were about seventy-five police officers as well as members of the fire department standing between the two groups. The protesters carried signs that named certain businesses whose practices were unfair. Standing five people deep on the sidewalk outside the courthouse, the demonstrators recited the Lord's Prayer, sang "God Bless America" and "We Shall Overcome," listened to a speech by Cox, and cheered him on. When they heard the twenty-three jailed protesters singing too, they cheered and applauded loudly.

As Cox's speech concluded, he instructed the crowd to head for sit-ins at the lunch counters: "It's lunchtime. Let's go eat. There are twelve stores we are protesting. A number of these stores have twenty counters; they accept your money from nineteen. They won't accept it from the twentieth counter. These stores are open to the public. You are members of the public. We pay taxes to the federal government and you who live here pay taxes to the state." The sheriff thought this speech was inflammatory, so he took the microphone from Cox and told the crowd to disperse. Some say Cox told his followers "Don't move," and others say he made a gesture of defiance. The crowd did not disperse. When the police fired tear gas at them, the protestors ran.

On December 16, Reverend Cox was arrested and then convicted for "willfully obstructing the public sidewalks, disturbing the peace, and picketing before a courthouse." (An additional charge of conspiracy did not hold.) On appeal, the state supreme court upheld the conviction. Cox then appealed his case to the U.S. Supreme Court, arguing that his conviction for a street protest was a violation of the First Amendment. Justice Arthur Goldberg articulated the Supreme Court's decision:

> It is clear to us that . . . Louisiana infringed [Cox's] rights of free speech and free assembly by convicting him under this [disturbing the peace] statute . . . Our independent examination of the record . . . shows no conduct which the State had a right to prohibit as a breach of the peace . . . Our conclusion that the record does not support the contention that the students' cheering, clapping, and singing consti-tuted a breach of the peace is confirmed by the fact that these were not relied on as a basis for conviction by the trial judge, who, rather, stated as his reason for convicting Cox of disturbing the peace that '[it] must be recognized to be inherently dangerous and a breach of the peace to bring 1,500 people, colored people, down in the predominantly white business district . . . and congregate across the street from the courthouse and sing songs as described to me by the defendant as the CORE national anthem, carrying

lines such as "black and white together" and to urge those 1,500 people to descend upon our lunch counters and sit there until they are served. That has to be an inherent breach of the peace' . . . Nor is there any evidence here of 'fighting words.'

In fact, the protest had been peaceful. Reporters had also captured it on film, so the Court had plenty of opportunities to see that Cox had only exercised his constitutional rights. In other words, the Supreme Court overturned the Louisiana verdict largely because it was clear that the judge's verdict stemmed from his racist beliefs. In addition, the Court found that the statute's first element, regarding breach of peace, was unspecific and far too broad. The Court also reversed the conviction of Cox under the "obstructing public passages" statute, showing that Baton Rouge's practices for regulating parades and meetings were unconstitutional. The officials in charge of such permits had been picking and choosing whose voice would be heard in the streets of Baton Rouge.

Marches

In August 1963, 250,000 people traveled to Washington, DC, to demand civil rights for all Americans. There were many speakers; Martin Luther King Jr. gave the closing address, his famous "I Have a Dream" speech. Though it took almost a year for a civil rights bill proposed by President Kennedy (the Civil Rights Act of 1964) to finally become law, the March on Washington had changed the country. Although the Civil Rights Act was significant in many ways, it had not done enough to help African

Americans, particularly in the South. When African Americans attempted to vote, they still were confronted by threats of violence and racist polling practices. In 1965, President Lyndon Johnson passed the Voting Rights Act. The Voting Rights Act gave the federal government the right to intervene when racial discrimination interfered with voting practices.

The Civil Rights movement had taught many Americans the power of speaking out for what they believed in—that their voices had possessed the power to change. Many people invoked the lessons of the Civil Rights movement in their protest against a war that they did not support—the war in Vietnam.

The Vietnam War

Vietnam, a country in Southeast Asia, has a long history of conflict with its neighbors, Thailand, Cambodia, Laos, and China. In 1954 the country was divided in two: Communist North Vietnam and nationalist South Vietnam. War broke out in South Vietnam as guerrillas led by the Communists, called the Viet Cong, tried to overthrow the South Vietnamese government.

As early as 1961, the United States began to supply troops to support South Vietnam. In 1964, after the North Vietnamese allegedly attacked an American destroyer, Congress gave President Lyndon Johnson the power to send as many troops to Vietnam as he saw fit. In 1965, U.S. forces began a massive bombing campaign against North Vietnam. As a result, the antiwar movement at home grew.

The war effort expanded rapidly. By 1969 there were approximately 550,000 American troops in Vietnam, fighting a war in unknown terrain—the jungle. At home, reports that the war was going well were soon discredited, which only fueled opposition to the war.

President Richard Nixon took office in 1973 after defeating Johnson. Nixon adopted a policy of increased bombing while at the same time withdrawing American ground forces. In 1973, a cease-fire agreement was signed between the two sides that allowed the remaining U.S. troops to return home. But the war did not really end until 1975, when the North Vietnamese defeated the southern army.

Birth of the Antiwar Movement

As the fighting in Vietnam unfolded, more and more Americans began to question the government's decision to send troops to Vietnam. Young people, angry about America's unnecessary involvement in the Vietnam War, began to demand answers. They wanted to know why the scheduled peace talks failed consistently and sought to understand why the troops were fighting. On many occasions, government reports about events in Vietnam were shown to be far from truthful. Also, news coverage revealed the gruesome and violent reality of war to Americans on a daily basis. In the meantime, more and more American soldiers died.

President Johnson also instituted the military draft. Registering for selective service is a part of the draft process.

The Vietnam War sparked an antiwar movement throughout the United States, motivating people to take to the streets in protest.

The selective service is mandatory service in the armed forces. When young men turn eighteen they are required to register with selective service. During the Vietnam War, registering was likely to result in becoming drafted, or placement in military service.

Students on college campuses, who were exempt from the draft because of their status as students, began to organize antiwar protests and events. Political organizations such as Students for a Democratic Society (SDS) held rallies and organized marches. Musicians took part in the cause, setting up concerts such as Woodstock, where they gave speeches and sang songs that expressed their feelings about the war. Rallies, marches, protests, demonstrations, and sit-ins were taking place all over the country. In 1970, an antiwar protest turned deadly when four students were shot and killed on the campus of Kent State University in Ohio.

Four Dead in Ohio

In May 1970, four students at Kent State University in Ohio were shot and killed by members of the National Guard. Eyewitness and gunshot victim Alan Canfora remembered some of the events that led up to the deaths of Allison Krause, Jeff Miller, Sandy Scheuer, and Bill Schroeder:

> On May 1, hundreds of angry antiwar students and some Vietnam veterans went on a rampage in downtown Kent. They did $5,000 worth of property damage. On May 3, Ohio governor James Rhodes arrived at Kent State, where he called the students "the worst type of people we harbor in America" and promised, "We're going to eradicate [violently remove] the problem." This only made the atmosphere at the school worse. Just a few hours later, Ohio National Guardsmen (ONG) attacked students with tear gas and rifles, injuring some students with the bayonets mounted on their rifles. By May 4, tensions were running high. Hundreds of ONG were on campus. Nearly 1,000 students held a peaceful rally on the campus Commons to protest the bombing of Cambodia.

"We assumed we still could exercise our constitutional rights of freedom of speech, freedom of assembly, and freedom to dissent," said Canfora. As the rally began, the ONG

The Rev. Daniel Berrigan (*right*) and his brother Philip were convicted of burning draft registration files to protest the Vietnam War. Here, newsmen interview Daniel Berrigan and his lawyer, William M. Kunstler.

The Berrigan Brothers

Daniel and Philip Berrigan are brothers, both Catholic priests, both activists. They garnered national attention when together they destroyed Vietnam War draft registration files in Catonsville, Maryland. They were each sentenced to three years in prison but went into hiding to avoid imprisonment. They were eventually caught and served some time in prison.

Both men have devoted their lives to peace. Daniel went to Hanoi, North Vietnam, to help win the release of three American pilots in 1968. He is also a poet and has written more than fifty books, including *Night Flight to Hanoi*. Philip has spoken out against the arms race and nuclear armament. He is a founding member of the Ploughshares group, which organizes nonviolent, direct actions against nuclear weapons manufacturers.

49

attacked, firing tear gas at the crowd. The students ran; the ONG followed. Some students and some Guardsmen threw rocks, but the two sides were too far away from each other for this to have any impact, so they stopped. Then a number of students walked toward the ONG, shouting angrily about the war and the behavior of these troops on campus. The ONG retreated up a hill. When they were some distance away, a number of them turned, took aim, and fired their M-1 rifles into the crowd of students for thirteen seconds.

Two of those students killed, Krause and Miller, were protesters. Scheuer and Schroeder were onlookers. The shots injured nine other students. None of the guardsmen were ever punished. Many accused President Nixon of creating an atmosphere in which it was acceptable to beat up and even murder antiwar protesters. This climate of suspicion was encouraged long before Nixon took office in 1969, however.

Tinker v. Des Moines (1969)

Also in 1969, a case concerning one young person's right to free speech reached the Supreme Court. A few years earlier, on December 16, 1965, eighth-grader Mary Beth Tinker wore a black armband to Warren Harding Junior High School in Des Moines, Iowa to express her opposition to the war in Vietnam. She attended her morning classes and went to lunch. After lunch, on her way to algebra class, she was called to the principal's office. Principal Pratt told Mary to take off her armband, which she did. Pratt then suspended her from school and sent her home. The Des Moines school board had ordered that no one could wear armbands to school, as they posed a threat to the peaceful operation of schools: "Any kind of demonstration might evolve into something difficult to control."

At Roosevelt High School, tenth-grader Chris Eckhardt was also suspended for wearing a black armband. Mary Tinker's father, a Methodist minister, called a meeting of students and parents to discuss the armband issue. They issued a statement indicating that the school board's denial of their children's opportunity to engage in this form of expression concerned them. Students had asked the school board to call an emergency meeting to discuss the ban, but the school board president argued that the issue was not important enough to warrant deviating from the meeting schedule. By the next day, three more Des Moines students had been suspended, including Mary's brother John, a tenth-grader at North High School. Interestingly, at these same schools, students had been allowed to wear buttons in support of a variety of political campaigns. Some students were even allowed to wear the Iron Cross, a Nazi symbol.

The Des Moines school board met and, after much heated debate, voted to keep the ban on armbands in place. The controversy did not end there. The Iowa Civil Liberties Union (ICLU), a state branch of the national organization, the ACLU, brought a suit against the Des Moines school board in federal court, seeking to lift the ban. But the judge considered the school board's policy reasonable, stating that although the students wearing armbands were peaceful, and there had been no evidence or complaint of any actual disturbance, the potential existed for *reactions to the armbands*. The board argued that these reactions might disturb regular school operations.

Still unsatisfied, the Tinkers took the case to the Supreme Court, where it was heard in November 1968. The case did not begin well; Justice Hugo Black had misunderstood the circumstances and had assumed that Mary had disrupted her algebra class. Allan Herrick, a lawyer representing the school board, tried to link Mary and the other suspended students with Students for a Democratic Society (SDS), pointing out that Chris and his mother had participated in an SDS-sponsored demonstration in Washington, DC. In the end, Mary Beth Tinker won. This case was an important victory for free speech and free expression advocates. Justice Abe Fortas delivered the Court's decision:

> [The wearing of armbands] was closely akin to "pure speech" which, we have repeatedly held, is entitled to comprehensive protection under the First Amendment . . . It can hardly be argued that either students or teachers shed their constitutional rights to freedom of speech or expression at the schoolhouse gate . . . Any variation from the majority's opinion may inspire fear. Any word spoken, in class, in the lunchroom, or on the campus, that deviates from the views of another person may start an argument or cause a disturbance. But our Constitution says we must take this risk. [The Court concluded that schools] may not be enclaves of totalitarianism.

Like Mary Beth Tinker, many Americans used their voices both figuratively and literally during the Civil Rights movement and the years of the Vietnam War. They put their faith in

Closeups of the Chicago Seven, from left to right: (top) Rubin, Hoffman, Hayden, Davis; (bottom) Seale, Weiner, Froines, and Dellinger

The Chicago Seven

Originally a group of eight, the Chicago Seven were political radicals brought to trial for conspiracy to incite a riot at the Democratic National Convention of 1968, which took place in Chicago. Many political organizations (although not the Black Panthers) had planned massive demonstrations during the convention. Chicago's Mayor Daley threatened to maintain order at all costs. As a result, crowd turnout was not as large as anticipated. About 10,000 demonstrators showed up and spent a week in violent confrontation with the police.

The Chicago Seven were Bobbie Seale (cofounder of the Black Panthers), John Froines and Lee Weiner (Chicago organizers), Abbie Hoffman and Jerry Rubin (leaders of the Youth International Party), Tom Hayden and Rennie Davis (leaders of Students for a Democratic Society), and David Dellinger (chairman of National Mobilization Against the War). With the exception of Seale, William Kunstler represented the defendants, who brought activists and singers into court to explain what the demonstrators were objecting to. Seale, whose behavior in court led to his being bound and gagged for three days, was sentenced to four years in jail for contempt of court after his case was declared a mistrial. In 1970, five of the remaining seven were found guilty, but this verdict was overturned in 1972. Judge Julius Hoffman was later found to have shown "overt hostility" toward the defendants and to have committed some procedural mistakes.

53

their constitutional right to speak against the government and to expect the government to respond. They made valuable statements about our right to say what we believe. They risked arrest and imprisonment, beatings, and even murder because they believed that "Congress shall make no law . . . abridging the freedom of speech."

Frisby v. Schultz (1988)

Two decades later, conservative and liberal protestors alike continued to employ these highly visible and effective ways of communicating their political opinions to a broad audience. In May 1985, the town of Brookfield, Wisconsin passed an antipicketing ordinance that placed a total ban on residential picketing. It stated that, "It is unlawful for any person to engage in picketing before or about the residence or dwelling of any individual in the town of Brookfield." Community leaders developed the ordinance in response to a group of antiabortion protesters that had picketed directly outside the home of Dr. Benjamin Victoria, a local doctor who performed abortions in a few nearby clinics. The group had picketed his house at least six times in the two months before the ordinance was passed.

Sandra Schultz was one of the picketers. When she realized that further picketing outside Dr. Victoria's house would end in her arrest, Schultz went to federal district court to sue Town Supervisor Russell Frisby. Schultz argued that the antipicketing ordinance was a violation of her First Amendment right to free speech. The ordinance was struck down by the district court, a verdict supported by the federal court of appeals, which called the ordinance "repugnant to the Constitution." On the surface, these courts appear to be correct. Schultz and her fellow protesters were exercising their right to free speech and their right to freedom of assembly, which gives Americans the opportunity to gather together in protest. The town of Brookfield then appealed the lower court's decision to the Supreme Court.

Back in 1985, the Supreme Court had decided in *Cornelius v. NAACP Legal Defense & Educational Fund, Inc.*, that there are three types of places in which the exercise of speech and expression are to be closely examined. They are the traditional public forum (such as a public street), a public forum designated by the government, and the nonpublic forum. Public streets have been considered traditionally a public forum. Frisby argued that the streets of Brookfield should be considered a nonpublic forum. He said streets that were residential and as physically narrow as Brookfield's have never been held open for public communication.

The Court rejected this idea, saying that "A public street does not lose its status as a traditional public forum simply because it runs through a residential neighborhood." The Court also concluded that Brookfield's ordinance was "content neutral," meaning that it does not discriminate against certain points of view, as Baton Rouge's parade policy did, in the case of Reverend Cox. In addition, the Court said a person's right not to be subjected to unwanted speech should be protected. The Brookfield ordinance does not ban picketing in residential neighborhoods. What it does ban is the targeting of a particular resident, "in an especially offensive way," and forcing that resident to hear unwanted speech.

Justice Sandra Day O'Connor delivered the Court's decision: "Because the picketing prohibited by the Brookfield ordinance is speech directed primarily at those who are presumptively unwilling to receive it, the State has a substantial and justifiable interest in banning it . . . The ordinance also leaves open ample alternative channels of communication and is content neutral. Thus, largely because of its narrow scope, the . . . challenge to the ordinance must fail. The contrary judgment of the Court of Appeals is reversed." The Supreme Court found that the value of being able to sit in one's home without being subjected to someone else's speech was sufficient to find the Brookfield ordinance acceptable under the Constitution.

In this and all cases, the courts consider the context within which speech is expressed. In legal cases involving free speech, judges examine where, when, why, and how ideas and opinions are communicated. After all, it is not only what one says but often what one does and where one does it that matters.

5 Obscenity

In 1957 in *Roth v. United States*, the Supreme Court ruled that "obscenity is not within the area of constitutionally protected speech or press." Justice William Brennan delivered the opinion of the court. In the Roth case, the constitutionality of the law that makes punishable the mailing of material that is "obscene, lewd, lascivious, or filthy . . . or other publication of an indecent character," was upheld

More often than not, obscenity is subjective. That is, not everyone agrees about what is obscene. Something that you might find offensive, another may find artistic. In the Roth case, the court also concluded that something could be called obscene if the average person would think that it really only appeals to people with an unusual amount of sexual interest, depicts sex in an offensive way, and lacks value—artistic, political, scientific, or literary. You may see a number of problems with this idea. For instance, who is the average person?

Private companies, such as television stations, have the right to refuse to televise shows that the station owner finds problematic. In 1997, in *Reno v. ACLU,* the Supreme Court ruled that television broadcasters and cable operators can block certain programs. For instance, even though the controversial *Howard Stern Show* is broadcast by the Columbia Broadcasting System (CBS) television network, you may not be able to see it if the cable operator in your town chooses to block that show.

Art and the City

In September 1999, an art exhibit at the Brooklyn Museum of Art in New York, called "Sensation: Young British Artists from the Saatchi Collection," featured explicit works such as a pig, cut in half and suspended in a tank of formaldehyde, and a bust of a man made from nine pints of his own frozen blood. It also featured a portrait of a Roman Catholic icon, the Virgin Mary, stained with elephant dung. The museum said it would not allow children under the age of seventeen to view the exhibit unless accompanied by an adult.

The mayor of New York, Rudolph Giuliani, threatened to close the museum. He was deeply offended by the painting of the Virgin Mary, as he is a Roman Catholic. He said the art exhibit was "sick stuff," and went on to explain why it did not qualify as art: "Anything that I can do isn't art. If I can do it, it's not art, because I'm not much of an artist. And I could figure out how to put this together. You know, if you want to throw dung at something, I could figure out how to do that."

The issue became more complicated as Giuliani demanded that the museum shut down the exhibit. When the museum refused, he turned to the museum's age-restriction policy for

Chris Ofili's *The Holy Virgin Mary,* was part of the Brooklyn Museum's "Sensation" exhibit in 1999, which offended New York mayor Rudy Giuliani, who tried to cut the museum's city funding.

"Sensation." Placing an age limit on admission to the show would violate the terms of the museum's lease, in a building owned by the city of New York. The lease states that museums housed in buildings owned by the city "shall at all reasonable times be free, open and accessible to the public and private schools" of the city, and "accessible to the general public on such terms of admission as the Mayor" sees fit. Giuliani pointed out, "Last time I checked, I'm the Mayor, and I don't find closing down access [to children under seventeen] to a public museum consistent with the use of taxpayer dollars. People have an absolute right to express anything they want to express, but they do not have an absolute right to have that [expression] funded by the taxpayer."

The Association of Art Museum Directors issued a statement in support of the exhibit: "Every art museum in this country is a center for the free exchange of ideas. If the Mayor acts on his intentions, it will set a precedent that could cripple museums across this country." The museum's director, Arnold Lehman, was confused by Giuliani's argument: "First we are told how vile and degenerate the exhibition is, and now we are being expected to open it up to children? The mayor is sending a mixed message." The city's corporation counsel, Michael Hess, said that the lease violation would not necessarily lead to closing the museum but to a change of the staff on the museum board.

Hess said new people would be hired who "would have better judgment as to what is appropriate for this type of museum." As the struggle between the mayor's office and the museum continued, Giuliani came up with yet another reason that the exhibit ought to be closed. "When it comes to Catholic bashing, this kind of thing is never treated as sensitively as it sometimes is in other areas. If this were a desecration of a symbol in another area, I think there would be more sensitivity about this than a desecration of a symbol that involves Catholics."

Giuliani believed that the show reflected a widespread acceptance of Catholic bashing. His mysterious comments about "another area," left some city residents wondering if he was bashing another group of people. The mayor was insistent about his point. "I'm not going to have any compunction about trying to put them out of business. Maybe that's the best way to preserve the museum and the good parts of the museum for everyone else."

Meanwhile, at the Whitney Museum, another museum in New York, an exhibit opened that contained a piece by artist Andres Serrano—a crucifix submerged in a jar of the artist's

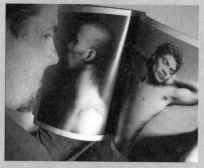

Robert Mapplethorpe (1946–1989)

Mapplethorpe was a famous American photographer whose work received much critical acclaim despite accusations that some of his photos were pornographic. He studied painting, drawing, and sculpture at the Pratt Institute of Art before turning to photography. His works include photos of gay men in sexually explicit positions, flowers, nudes, and portraits of celebrities. He exhibited his work in Paris, New York, and Washington, DC. When there was an exhibit of his photos at the Contemporary Arts Center in Cincinnati, Ohio, the director of the center was arrested and tried on obscenity charges. Ultimately, he was acquitted.

urine. The mayor's office made no move to close that show, as the Whitney is not in a city-owned building, and the museum had not received any funds from the city that year.

The Mayor's Day in Court

When Giuliani took his case against the Brooklyn Museum to U.S. district court, he lost. Federal judge Nina Gershon said that Giuliani had violated the First Amendment when he cut off city funds to the museum and began eviction proceedings against it. Gershon ordered the mayor and New York City to restore funding to the museum and to stop all attempts to evict the museum from its building or to interfere with the museum's board in any way. In her decision, she wrote that the city's court case was "conceived and initiated . . . to pressure the museum" and that it is "part of an ongoing effort to retaliate against and deter [the museum's] exercise of First Amendment rights." Gershon also rejected the city's request to put its monthly payments to the museum (averaging about $500,000) into an escrow account while it appealed her decision. She ordered the city to pay the museum immediately.

Regarding the museum's First Amendment rights, Gershon went on to say, "There is no federal constitutional issue more grave than the effort by government officials to censor works of expression and to threaten the vitality of a major cultural institution, as punishment for failing to abide by governmental demands for orthodoxy." The court's decision also clarified the question of funding. The city was not asked to fund "Sensation"; the city's money was used for building maintenance, the salaries of museum employees, and other expenses, such as heating, cooling, and lighting. With regard to Giuliani's claim that the artworks are sacrilegious and therefore in support of "anti-Catholic" views, Gershon pointed out that the same museum also houses many other works that venerate religious figures, including the Virgin Mary. The controversy did not end there.

In February 2001, the museum opened an exhibit of 188 photographs by ninety-four black photographers. One of the photographs was a fifteen-foot panel called *Yo' Mama's Last Supper*, by Renée Cox. In it, the artist is portrayed as a nude Christ, surrounded by twelve black apostles. Giuliani called the exhibit "disgusting," "outrageous," and "anti-Catholic." Cox, whose photograph has been shown elsewhere without any controversy said, "Get over it. I don't produce work that necessarily looks good over somebody's couch."

Giuliani declared that he would do everything in his power to set up a decency committee to set standards for museums that receive public money, and he hoped to bring his case before the Supreme Court. Although obscenity objections arise frequently about art exhibits and entertainment endeavors, obscene speech in schools became the subject of a Supreme Court case in the 1980s.

Bethel School District v. Fraser (1986)

Matthew Fraser was a student at Bethel High School in Bethel, Washington. On April 26, 1983, he gave a speech to nominate a fellow student for an office in student government. His speech contained a number of sexual metaphors, including the following:

> I know a man who is firm—he's firm in his pants, he's firm in his shirt, his character is firm—but most . . . of all, his belief in you, the students of Bethel, is firm . . . Jeff Kulman is a man who takes his point and pounds it in. If necessary, he'll take an issue and nail it to the wall. He doesn't attack things in spurts—he drives hard, pushing and pushing until finally—he succeeds . . . Jeff is a man who will go to the very end—even the climax, for each and every one of you . . . So vote for Jeff for A.S.B. vice president—he'll never come between you and the best our high school can be.

The Right to Free Speech

Students reacted in a variety of ways during Fraser's speech. Some hooted and yelled. Some mimicked the sexual activities alluded to in the speech, and others appeared to be bewildered and embarrassed by the speech. The assembly at which Fraser gave this speech was attended by about 600 students, age fourteen to eighteen, all of whom were required to be there, unless they chose study hall instead. Before the assembly, Fraser had discussed his speech with three teachers, two of whom told him that "he probably should not deliver it," as it contained "explicit sexual metaphor." The teachers also informed Fraser that the speech could have "severe consequences." Bethel High School does have a disciplinary rule forbidding the use of obscene language in the school which states: "Conduct which materially and substantially interferes with the educational process is prohibited, including the use of obscene, profane language or gestures." Significantly, none of the teachers Fraser spoke with told him that his speech might violate a school rule.

The next morning, Fraser was called to the assistant principal's office. The assistant principal informed him that his speech had violated the school rule against obscene language. Fraser admitted to having deliberately used sexual innuendo in his speech. The assistant principal suspended Fraser for three days and told him he would not be eligible to speak at graduation ceremonies at the end of the year.

Fraser went to the school's hearing officer to review the school's action. The hearing officer said that Fraser's speech was "indecent, lewd, and offensive to the modesty and decency of many of the students and faculty in attendance at the assembly." Fraser served two days of his suspension and was allowed to return to school on the third day.

Meanwhile, E. L. Fraser, Fraser's father, took issue with the school's actions and brought the case to the federal district court, arguing that the school had violated his son's First Amendment right to free speech. Fraser's father argued further that because the school's disciplinary code said nothing about suspension as a punishment, the school had also violated his son's Fourteenth Amendment right to due process. The district court agreed with the Frasers, who won damages as well as Matthew Fraser's right to speak at commencement, which he did, on June 8, 1983.

The school district appealed the district court's decision. The court of appeals upheld the judgment of the district court, even as the school district argued that Fraser's speech had "a disruptive effect on the educational process." The school district also argued that it was trying to protect an "essentially captive audience of minors from lewd and indecent language in a setting sponsored by the school." Finally, in 1986 the Supreme Court, however, ruled that the student's free speech rights had not been violated. The verdict was read by Chief Justice Warren Burger:

> This Court acknowledged in *Tinker v. Des Moines* that students do not 'shed their constitutional rights to freedom of speech or expression at the schoolhouse gate.' The Court did not recognize, however, that making an obscene nominating speech was essentially the same as the wearing of an armband . . . as a form of protest or the expression of a political position . . . The objectives of public education [are] the 'inculcation of fundamental values necessary to the maintenance of a democratic political system' . . . The undoubted freedom to advocate unpopular and

controversial views in schools and classrooms must be balanced against the society's countervailing interest in teaching students the boundaries of socially appropriate behavior. Even the most heated political discourse in a democratic society requires consideration for the personal sensibilities of the other participants and audiences . . . The First Amendment guarantees wide freedom in matters of adult public discourse . . . It does not follow, however, that simply because the use of an offensive form of expression may not be prohibited to adults making what the speaker considers a political point, the same latitude must be permitted to children in a public school . . . As cogently expressed by Judge Newman, 'the first amendment gives a high school student the classroom right to wear Tinker's armband, but not Cohen's jacket.' [You will read about *Cohen v. California* next.] . . . The determination of what manner of speech in the classroom or in school assembly is inappropriate properly rests with the school board . . . we hold that . . . [the] School District acted entirely within its permissible authority in imposing sanctions upon Fraser in response to his offensively lewd and indecent speech. Unlike the sanctions imposed on the students wearing armbands in *Tinker*, the penalties imposed in this case were unrelated to any political viewpoint.

In other words, Fraser's speech was not protected because he was not being punished for expressing an opinion, but for the way he expressed it. That is, he was not punished for nominating his candidate; he was punished for how he nominated his candidate.

Cohen v. California (1971)

Interestingly, nearly two decades prior to the Fraser case, the Supreme Court confronted the intersection of political speech and obscenity. On April 26, 1968, Paul Cohen was arrested for breaking California's Vulgar Speech Law: "Every person who maliciously and willfully disturbs the peace or quiet by offensive conduct or the use of any vulgar, profane, or indecent language shall be guilty of a misdemeanor." Cohen was in a public place, the Los Angeles County courthouse, wearing a jacket with the words "F— the Draft" printed on it. He said he wore the jacket to express the way he felt about the selective service system and America's involvement in the Vietnam War.

In the Los Angeles County Municipal Court, he was found guilty and sentenced to thirty days in jail. When Cohen appealed the court's ruling, the California Court of Appeals upheld the verdict. The California Supreme Court declined to hear the case.

Cohen then requested a hearing with the U.S. Supreme Court, claiming that California had violated his rights by punishing him for displaying an antiwar message; he argued that his four-letter-word protest was protected by the First Amendment. (The court argued that the term "offensive conduct" can refer to "behavior which has a tendency to provoke others to acts of violence or to in turn disturb the peace.") Justice John Marshall Harlan announced the Court's decision:

The conviction quite clearly rests upon the asserted offensiveness of the words Cohen used to convey his message to the public. The only "conduct" which the state sought to punish is the fact of communication. Thus, we deal here with a conviction resting solely upon 'speech,' not upon any separately identifiable conduct which allegedly was intended by Cohen to be perceived by others as expressive of particular views but which . . . does not necessarily convey any message and hence arguably could be regulated without effectively repressing Cohen's ability to express himself.

The Supreme Court argued that the State could not punish Cohen for the underlying content or meaning of his message, as long as there was no obvious intent to disrupt the operation of the selective service or to encourage others to disobey the law. The Court held that the case was not about where he had worn the jacket (in the Los Angeles County courthouse), nor was it about obscenity, as there was nothing sexual about the words on the jacket. It was also not a case of "fighting words," as the message was not "directed to the person or the hearer," that is, not to anyone in particular with whom Cohen might start a fight. The state maintained that it acted as it did "to protect the sensitive from otherwise unavoidable exposure to [Cohen's] crude form of protest."

The Court noted, however, that "persons confronted with Cohen's jacket were in a quite different posture than, say, those subjected to the raucous emissions of sound from trucks blaring outside their residences. Those in the Los

Angeles County courthouse could effectively avoid further bombardment of their sensibilities simply by averting their eyes." The Justices realized that if Cohen's speech were protected, the fact that some of his listeners in a public building might be unwillingly exposed to it does not justify Cohen's conviction for breach of peace.

The California court's fear of disturbance was not sufficient cause to remove Cohen's right of free expression. There was no evidence, either, that any kind of unrest took place as a result of the jacket. Justice Harlan concluded:

> That the air may at times seem filled with verbal cacophony is, in this sense, not a sign of weakness but of strength . . . 'So long as the means are peaceful, the communication need not meet standards of acceptability' . . . While the particular four-letter word being litigated here is perhaps more distasteful than most others of its genre, it is nevertheless often true that one man's vulgarity is another man's lyric . . . Linguistic expression . . . conveys not only ideas capable of relatively precise, detached explication, but otherwise inexpressible emotions as well . . .

And Justice Felix Frankfurter concluded:

> One of the prerogatives of American citizenship is the right to criticize public men and measures— and that means not only informed and responsible criticism but also the freedom to speak foolishly and without moderation' . . .We cannot indulge

the . . . assumption that one can forbid particular words without also running a substantial risk of suppressing ideas in the process . . . It is . . . our judgment that . . . the State may not, consistently with the First and Fourteenth Amendments, make the simple public display here involved of this single four-letter expletive a criminal offense . . . The judgment [of the California Court of Appeal] must be reversed.

As Cohen's case illustrates, speech takes many forms, both verbal and nonverbal. In fact, symbolic speech has long been contested in the courts.

6 Symbolic Speech

There are many kinds of symbolic speech. Paul Cohen's jacket conveyed a very direct, but nonverbal message. Other forms of speech stress actions as much, if not more, than words, such as marches, demonstrations, and the sit-ins of the Civil Rights movement and the Vietnam War era. All of these were forms not only of protest but also of symbolic, or non-verbal speech. This chapter focuses on a number of important Supreme Court cases (and one from the court of appeals) that explicitly address the concept of symbolic speech, from saluting a flag to wearing a seemingly unconventional hairstyle.

Stromberg v. California (1931)

In 1928, nineteen-year-old Yetta Stromberg was charged and convicted of breaking a California law that stated:

> Any person who displays a red flag, banner, or badge or any flag, badge, banner, or device of any

color or form whatever in any public place or in any meeting place or public assembly, or from or on any house, building, or window as a sign, symbol, or emblem of opposition to organized government or as an invitation or stimulus to anarchistic action or as an aid to propaganda that is of a seditious character is guilty of a felony.

The law consisted basically of three elements: a flag as a symbol of opposition to the government, an invitation to anarchistic action, and an aid to seditious propaganda.

Stromberg was a member of the Young Communist League, an international organization that had ties to the Communist Party. She was also one of the supervisors of a summer camp for children between the ages of ten and fifteen in the San Bernardino Mountains. She taught history and economics to the campers. More specifically, she taught her students to become more class-conscious, to favor the solidarity of workers. She maintained that workers were united by blood, and were brothers and sisters in class struggle.

The charges brought against Stromberg centered on one of the camp's daily activities. Stromberg taught and led the children in a flag-raising ceremony. They raised a red flag, one made at the camp that was a reproduction of the flag of the Communist Party in the United States. The children stood, saluted the flag, and recited a pledge of allegiance to the red flag, and "to the cause for which it stands, one aim throughout our lives, freedom for the working class."

The camp library also contained many books and pamphlets that espoused radical communist dogma. California state officials argued that these books and pamphlets contained "incitements to violence and to armed uprisings, teaching the indispensability of a desperate, bloody, destructive war as the immediate task of the coming action." Stromberg did own some of these books, but she said they were not used for teaching at the camp, nor could it be proved that they were used to that end. She also claimed that she did not use words "fostering sedition" or "anarchy" in her teaching of the children.

Stromberg was convicted by the Superior Court of San Bernardino County. She appealed the decision in the California District Court of Appeals, petitioned for a hearing by the Supreme Court of California and was denied. She then brought her appeal before the U.S. Supreme Court. During her district court of appeals case, Stromberg argued that the California statute under which she had been convicted was unconstitutional. She insisted that "under the Fourteenth Amendment, the statute was invalid as being 'an unwarranted limitation on the right of free speech.'"

The Fourteenth Amendment is designed to protect us from state laws that are unconstitutional. Strangely, although the California law specifies three purposes it intends to serve, the verdict against Stromberg never said on which of the three her conviction rested. Regardless, if the Supreme Court found the law unconstitutional, Stromberg's conviction could not be upheld.

The Supreme Court, then, examined the California statute. Their decision was as follows:

It has been determined that the conception of liberty under the due process clause of the Fourteenth Amendment embraces the right of free speech. The right is not an absolute one, and the State in the exercise of its police power may punish the abuse of this freedom. There is no question . . . that the State may . . . provide for the punishment of those who indulge in utterances which incite to violence and crime and threaten the overthrow of organized government by unlawful means . . . We have no reason to doubt the validity of the second and third clauses of the statute ["invitation to action" and "aid to seditious propaganda"] as construed by the state court to relate to such incitements to violence . . .

The question is thus narrowed to the validity of the first clause [symbol of opposition]. A statute which upon its face . . . is so vague and indefinite as to permit the punishment of the fair use of this opportunity is repugnant to the guaranty of liberty contained in the Fourteenth Amendment. The first clause of the statute being invalid . . . the conviction of [Stromberg], which so far as the record discloses may have rested upon that clause exclusively, must be set aside.

Stromberg's conviction was overturned because the Supreme Court realized that the first part of the California law was unconstitutional. The government may not make opposition to itself illegal. In fact, the point of the free speech clause of the First Amendment is to protect our right to oppose the government. This next case also involved a flag, but this time it was the United States flag.

Minersville v. Gobitis (1940)

Dear Sirs

I do not salute the flag because I have promised to do the will of God. That means that I must not worship anything out of harmony with God's law. In the twentieth chapter of Exodus it is stated, "Thou shalt not make unto thee any graven image, nor bow down to them nor serve them for I the Lord thy God am a jealous God visiting the iniquity of the fathers upon the children unto the third and fourth generation of them that hate me." I am a true follower of Christ. I do not salute the flag not because I do not love my country, but I love my country and I love God more and I must obey His commandments.

Your pupil,
Billy Gobitas

Billy Gobitas wrote this letter to school officials in Minersville, Pennsylvania on November 5, 1935. A court clerk mistakenly mispelled the family's last name, changing it from Gobitas to Gobitis—it stuck.

Billy's family belonged to the Jehovah's Witnesses, a religious sect not particularly popular in Minersville, where nearly 90 percent of the population was Roman Catholic. The Gobitas family did not become Witnesses until 1931, and at school, the Gobitas children saluted the flag until 1935.

Refusing to salute the flag was no small matter during this era. After World War I American veterans formed an organization called the American Legion. The Legion began a campaign. As noted in Peter Irons' *The Courage of Their Convictions: Sixteen Americans Who Fought Their Way to the Supreme Court,* their general goal was "100 percent Americanism." This was a thinly veiled reactionary campaign against ethnic and racial minorities. They were joined eventually by the Veterans of Foreign Wars (VFW), the Daughters of the American Revolution (DAR), and the Ku Klux Klan (KKK). At the time, the Klan was trying to upgrade its image by aligning itself with so-called patriotic causes. By 1935, eighteen states had adopted flag-salute statutes. Hundreds of school boards across the country jumped on the patriotic bandwagon, voting to add the flag ceremony as a mandatory part of their curriculum.

According to Peter Irons "In 1935, Jehovah's Witnesses became the first religious group to promote a campaign of refusal to join classroom ceremonies, and to press their challenges in court on a constitutional basis." The Witnesses' refusal to salute the flag in Nazi Germany (and general refusal to be worshipful of the state) landed more than 10,000 Witnesses in concentration camps during World War II (1939–1945).

Reacting to the experience of the German Jehovah's Witnesses, the leader of the American Witnesses, Joseph Rutherford, spoke against flag-saluting laws at the sect's national convention. Witnesses, he said, "do not 'Heil Hitler' or any other creature." Just a few days after Rutherford's speech, the Gobitas children, Lillian and Billy, decided they would not salute the flag. They could not be punished for

Jehovah's Witnesses and Free Speech

The Jehovah's Witnesses organization has, in its history, argued in court a great deal for free speech rights. Consequently, it has managed to solidify protection of our First Amendment rights. According to religion and law scholar Eric Michael Mazur in his book *The Americanization of Religious Minorities: Confronting the Constitutional Order,* "From 1938 to 1960, more than fifty cases involving members of the [Jehovah's Witnesses] organization reached the Supreme Court, producing more than thirty separate decisions on issues from flag-saluting to colportage [selling or distributing religious books]." The Jehovah's Witnesses believe that the only authority to which its members answer is God, and that all earthly governments would be overthrown by God. Such a belief system sets the stage for conflict with the federal government.

An early encounter with constitutional law took place in 1918, when the organization's then-president, Joseph Rutherford, was arrested for violating the Espionage Act of 1917. He was found guilty in federal district court of publishing (and distributing) materials that encouraged readers to resist the draft. However, the verdict was reversed by the federal court of appeals.

Other court cases involving the Jehovah's Witnesses' struggle to exercise their right to free speech (and freedom of the press) include:

- *Lovell v. City of Griffin* (1938) — protection of the right to distribute literature
- *Minersville v. Gobitis* (1940) — lost the right to refuse to salute the American flags in schools
- *Jones v. Opelika* (1943) — limits speech that might cause "a breach of the peace"
- *Jamison v. Texas* (1943) — the right to distribute printed material
- *Murdock v. Pennsylvania* (1943) — protection of colportage

- West Virginia Board of Ed. v. Barnette (1943) — right of free speech includes the right not to say what we do not believe, such as the Pledge of Allegiance
- Wooley v. Maynard (1977) — right not to support an ideology

Eventually, changes in the organization's interpretation of Scripture slowed the occurrence of their regular appearances before the Supreme Court, as laws seen as "good," as protecting their rights, could and should be obeyed. The Witnesses' role in winning the protection of our right to free speech should not be underestimated.

this defiance, as neither the school nor the state had yet made the salute a requirement.

At the urging of school superintendent Charles Roudabush, the school board met, and they unanimously adopted a resolution that made the daily flag salute mandatory. Any refusal on the part of a student to take part in this ritual would "be regarded as an act of insubordination and [would] be dealt with accordingly." Roudabush wasted no time in expelling the Gobitas children from the Minersville schools.

At the Courthouse

More than a year later, Walter Gobitas, Billy's father took the school board to federal district court. He was represented by the American Civil Liberties Union (ACLU) and Witness lawyers from the sect's New York headquarters. His complaint raised the issue of due process under the Fourteenth Amendment. Section one of the Fourteenth Amendment forbids the states from abridging or denying the privileges and immunities of U.S. citizens, to deprive any person of life, liberty, or property without due process of law, and to deny any person the equal protection of the law. In the early days of the Supreme Court, a deprivation of "life, liberty, or property" typically referred to the punishment for crime. Due process would be observed by following fair procedures, including providing the defendant an open trial and the right to counsel. In time, however, the court concluded that due process was not limited to procedure. Even if proper legal procedures were observed, the grounds on which a person was deprived of his or her rights to life, liberty, or property might violate due process. The constitutionality of many state laws was thus opened to question.

Dozens of Supreme Court cases, dating from the 1890s, on matters of speech, religion, and assembly demonstrate that state and local governments are not allowed to limit any First Amendment rights that Congress would guarantee. The school board's argument was that saluting the flag was not a religious ceremony, but simply part of the curriculum meant to inculcate patriotism in the students. The board claimed it was protecting the health, safety, welfare, and morals of school students.

The judge assigned to the case, Albert Maris, noted that the Pennsylvania state constitution's protection of rights of conscience was at issue. In drafting its constitution in 1776, Pennsylvania wanted to broaden the scope of the First Amendment, and so the notion of rights of conscience had been included to expand protection of individual liberties. The 1776 state constitution holds that "all men have a natural and unalienable right to worship Almighty God according to the dictates of their own consciences and understanding . . . And that no authority can or ought to be vested in, or assumed by any power whatever, that shall in any case interfere with, or in any manner control, the right of conscience in the free exercise of religious worship." Consequently, in Maris's final opinion, he defended the rights of the individual over those of the group. He stated that it was "clear from the evidence that the refusal of these two earnest Christian children to salute the flag cannot even remotely prejudice or imperil the safety, health, morals, property or personal rights of their fellows." He ordered that the Gobitas children should be readmitted to the school with no requirement to participate in the flag salute.

The school board appealed this decision. The U.S. Court of Appeals upheld Maris's verdict. The judge in that case said, "Eighteen big states have seen fit to exert their power over a small number of little children . . . [The mandatory flag ceremony] happens to be abhorrent to the particular love of God of the little girl and boy now seeking our protection."

The Supreme Court Decision

The board appealed again, and the case went before the U.S. Supreme Court in 1940. Members of the ACLU and leader of the American Witnesses, Joseph Rutherford, testified on behalf of the Gobitas children. The Supreme Court found in favor of the Minersville school board. Possibly influenced by the oncoming threat of global war, the court was moved to a show of patriotism by a vote of eight to one. Justice Felix Frankfurter wrote the Court's opinion that although "every possible leeway should be given to the claims of religious faith . . . [religion] does not relieve the citizen from the discharge of political responsibilities." Frankfurter felt that the Supreme Court should not "exercise [its] judicial power unduly," by holding "too tight a rein" on state and local authorities.

Dissenting Justice Harlan Fiske Stone argued that laws that limit or put restrictions on personal liberties are generally aimed at "politically helpless minorities." He held that the Constitution should certainly win out over "popular government," that is, state and local governments. This issue continues to divide the Court to this day.

At the end of this battle, however, the fight had only just begun. Within two weeks of the Court's decision, Witnesses were attacked all over the country. These attacks, some of them truly horrifying, continued for two years after the case, decreasing in number only when America's attention had been diverted to the war in Europe and the Pacific. The Court came under much fire from scholars and journalists, and a number of justices looked forward to a time when they would be able to reverse the *Minersville v. Gobitis* decision. They found that opportunity a short time later.

West Virginia Board of Ed. v. Barnette (1943)

In 1943, the Supreme Court agreed to hear the case of three children who lived near Charleston, West Virginia. Walter Barnette, Lucy McClure, and Paul Stull had been expelled from school because of the state board of education's flag-salute policy. The Supreme Court's opinion took careful aim at Justice Frankfurter's refusal to protect a person's First

Amendment rights from the actions of local officials and electoral majorities. Frankfurter had said that civil obligations outweighed religious convictions. Justice Robert Jackson delivered the Court's decision:

> The Witnesses are an unincorporated body teaching that the obligation imposed by the law of God is superior to that of laws enacted by temporal government . . . Children of this faith have been expelled from school and are threatened with exclusion for no other cause. Officials threaten to send them to reformatories maintained for criminally inclined juveniles. Parents of such children have been prosecuted and are threatened with prosecutions for causing delinquency . . . There is no doubt that, in connection with pledges, the flag salute is a form of utterance. Symbolism is a primitive but effective way of communicating ideas . . . A person gets from a symbol the meaning he puts into it, and what is one man's comfort and inspiration is another man's jest and scorn . . . It is also to be noted that the compulsory flag salute and pledge requires affirmation of a belief and an attitude of mind.

Jackson argued that symbols mean different things to different people. Jackson was trying to contextualize the use of the U.S. flag as a symbol of patriotism. He notes that symbols are used to unite causes, nations, and political parties, and that the state and churches speak through such symbols. Acceptance of the meaning of a symbol usually involves a form of participation in it, some action to show one's belief. Jackson continued:

> It is now a commonplace that censorship or suppression of expression of opinion is tolerated by our Constitution only when it presents a clear and present danger of action of a kind the State is empowered to prevent and punish . . . But here the power of compulsion is invoked without any allegation that remaining passive during a flag salute ritual creates a clear and present danger that would justify an effort even to muffle expression . . . To sustain the compulsory flag salute we are required to say that a Bill of Rights which guards the individual's right to speak his own mind, left it open to public authorities to compel him to utter what is not in his mind.

In this decision, the Court reminds us that clear and present danger would be speech or actions that threaten the state, that actually risk governmental overthrow. It is obvious that small children refusing to salute a flag are unlikely to bring an end to America's present form of government. In addition, the Court points out, forcing people to salute the flag nullifies the Bill of Rights. It is tantamount to forcing us to say things we do not believe instead of exercising our right to speak about what we believe or to choose silence.

> [The] validity of the asserted power to force an American citizen publicly to profess any statement of belief or to engage in any ceremony of assent to

83

one, presents questions of power that must be considered independently of any idea we may have as to the utility of the ceremony in question . . . Free public education, if faithful to the ideal of secular instruction and political neutrality, will not be partisan or enemy of any class, creed, party, or faction . . . the very purpose of the Bill of Rights was to withdraw certain subjects from the vicissitudes of political controversy, to place them beyond the reach of majorities and officials and to establish them as legal principles to be applied by the courts. One's right to life, liberty, and property, to free speech, a free press, freedom of worship and assembly, and other fundamental rights may not be submitted to vote; they depend on the outcome of no elections.

An individual's belief system is not to be determined by a popular vote—in other words, even if the majority believes that we should salute the flag, it is not allowed to use its size and power to force the minority to participate.

This decision also illustrates that the Supreme Court itself is not immune to politics and current events. The country had to remain unified in its fight against Hitler; public support helps to win wars. If Hitler was killing dissenters, (and he most certainly was) then punishing dissent was seen as entirely un-American.

Struggles to coerce uniformity of sentiment in support of some end thought essential to their time and country have been waged by many good as well as evil men . . . Probably no deeper division of our people could proceed from any provocation than from finding it necessary to choose what doctrine and whose program public educational officials shall compel youth to unite in embracing. The ultimate futility of such attempts to compel coherence is the lesson of every such effort from the Roman drive to stamp out Christianity as a disturber of its pagan unity . . . to the fast failing efforts of our present totalitarian enemies [Hitler and Nazism]. Those who begin coercive elimination of dissent soon find themselves exterminating dissenters. Compulsory unification of opinion achieves only the unanimity of the graveyard.

Finally, the Court concludes, "Freedom to differ is not limited to things that do not matter much . . . the test of [freedom's] substance is the right to differ as to things that touch the heart of the existing order . . . we think the action of the local authorities in compelling the flag salute and pledge transcends constitutional limitations on their power and invades the sphere of intellect and spirit which it is the purpose of the First Amendment to our Constitution to reserve from all official control . . . the decision of this Court in *Minersville School District v. Gobitis* [and similar cases that came before it] are overruled."

United States v. O'Brien (1968)

This case focuses on another symbolic act—a young man burning his draft card. On March 31, 1966, there was a large Vietnam War protest outside a courthouse in South Boston, Massachusetts. One of the protesters, David O'Brien, publicly set fire to his draft card. A draft card is a certificate that verifies a person's registration with the selective service. The Federal Bureau of Investigation (FBI) arrested and brought O'Brien to trial under a 1965 amendment to the Selective Service Act. The Universal Military Training and Service Act, a federal law, required all men between the ages of eighteen and twenty-six to register for service in the military.

Conscription, or required military registration, became a major social issue during the Vietnam War era. There were many demonstrations at draft boards and induction centers. Many people evaded the draft; thousands fled the country or went to prison. The amendment, or addition, to this act that O'Brien was accused of violating reads: "Anyone who forges, alters, or knowingly destroys or knowingly mutilates a Selective Service Registration Certificate will be subject to a fine of not more than $10,000 or imprisonment of not more than ten years."

O'Brien did not deny that he had burned his draft card. In fact, he told the FBI agents that he had done so to express his beliefs; he knowingly broke a federal law. In the U.S. District Court, he said the 1965 amendment was a violation of his First Amendment right to free speech. He had burned the card, he said, "so that other people would reevaluate their positions with Selective Service, with the armed forces, and reevaluate their place in the culture of today, to hopefully consider my position."

Nevertheless, the Federal District Court decided that the Selective Service Act Amendment was indeed constitutional—

and they found O'Brien guilty. He appealed the decision to the U.S. Court of Appeals, which overturned his conviction and declared the 1965 amendment to be unconstitutional. The Department of Justice appealed the decision to overturn O'Brien's conviction to the United States Supreme Court. Chief Justice Earl Warren announced the court's decision:

> We hold that the 1965 Amendment is constitutional both as enacted and as applied. We therefore [throw out] the judgment of the Court of Appeals and reinstate the judgment and sentence of the District Court . . . we note at the outset that the 1965 Amendment plainly does not abridge free speech . . . [it] deals with conduct having no connection with speech. It prohibits the knowing destruction of certificates issued by the Selective Service System, and there is nothing necessarily expressive about such conduct.

Just twenty-five years after the *Barnette* case, the Warren court reinterpreted the notion of symbolism. The justices viewed the act of burning the draft card as just that—an act. The amendment to the Selective Service Act prohibits knowingly destroying the card, and says nothing about speech. Warren approached the issue with a very literal and conservative interpretation of speech.

> The amendment does not distinguish between public and private destruction, and it does not punish only destruction engaged in for the purpose of expressing views. A law prohibiting destruction

of Selective Service certificates no more abridges free speech . . . than a motor vehicle law prohibiting the destruction of drivers' licenses.

Again, Warren's reading of the amendment is narrow; he sees no relationship between the prohibitions in it and the right of free speech. O'Brien argued that the amendment was unconstitutional because of the way it was used to convict him—it was used, he said, "to suppress freedom of speech." O'Brien maintained that what he did was protected as symbolic speech, and that "the freedom of expression which the First Amendment guarantees includes all modes of 'communication of ideas by conduct,' and that his conduct was within this definition because he did it in 'demonstration against the war and against the draft.'"

The Court went on to say, "We cannot accept the view that an apparently limitless variety of conduct can be labeled 'speech' whenever the person engaging in the conduct intends thereby to express an idea . . . This Court has held that when 'speech' and 'nonspeech' elements are combined in the same course of conduct, a sufficiently important governmental interest in regulating the nonspeech element can justify incidental limitations on First Amendment freedoms." The Warren court insisted on drawing the line somewhere. Otherwise, no actions would be unlawful.

The Court also listed a variety of purposes that a draft card serves that would necessarily be limited by the destruction of the card. The Court's reasoning also reveals the possibility of a politically influenced verdict: "We think it also apparent that the Nation has a vital interest in having a system for raising armies that function with maximum

Former Supreme Court Chief Justice Earl Warren wrote the decision in the O'Brien case that supported laws that banned the burning of draft cards.

efficiency and is capable of easily and quickly responding to continually changing circumstances." At the time of this trial, the war in Vietnam was escalating, with the United States sending more and more troops into Asia. In the Court's opinion, the governmental interest in making sure it could draft O'Brien and others holding draft cards is sufficient to justify his conviction—he interfered with the operation of the selective service. The Court concluded that if government interest is valid and important, unrelated to the suppression of free speech, then the government can regulate conduct no more than is necessary to further that interest.

The Court then turned its attention to O'Brien's contention that the amendment was unconstitutional due to Congress' purpose in passing it. O'Brien argued that Congress wanted to suppress free speech. The justices did not agree that legislative motive in this case was an acceptable reason to declare this statute unconstitutional, and they pointed out that there was almost no Congressional debate over the amendment. The bill had passed by a vote of 393 to 1 in Congress. The Court reinstated the judgment against O'Brien, basing its decision mostly on the notion that destroying a draft card would disrupt the smooth functioning of the selective service system.

Like the O'Brien case, other court cases involving issues of free speech have assessed not only the way speech is expressed, they have also considered if the underlying idea itself warrants protection. Recently, a number of cases have focused on this very issue.

7

Hate Speech

Unfortunately, there are many prejudiced people in America who discriminate against women, racial minorities, and gays and lesbians. These people have been known to share their views, no matter how distasteful. The expression of their views is often described as hate speech. Some First Amendment scholars argue that hate speech ought to be censored because it hurts the targeted person or group of people on an emotional and psychological level. Moreover, hate speech diminishes the community or social standing of the targeted group, often promulgating negative stereotypes.

This strategy raises many vexing issues. After all, placing limits on speech is difficult. Who decides precisely what the speech means and how it is received? How would limits be enforced? What kinds of words are threatening, intimidating, or harassing, and, therefore, subject to legal action?

Hate Speech on the Internet

Unfortunately, many sites on the Internet contain hate speech and promote hating others. Their numbers are growing. In 1999, the Simon Wiesenthal Center, a research and educational organization, published *Digital Hate 2000,* an interactive report on hate on the Internet. The danger of these Web sites, the center points out, is how easy it is for hate propaganda to disguise itself online. A personal home page may look as though it merely discusses the page's designer, or a city. It may appear to provide historical information about an important figure. These homepages are often just a click or two away from angry, often racist speech, however. In fact, some sites offer computer games that have been reconfigured to include members of minority groups as the targets.

Is it possible or imperative for these sites to be subject to the law? There is no clear answer, especially because there is no ultimate gatekeeper of the Internet. Some advocate the censorship of hate messages on the Web, but others, such as members of the ACLU, argue for the protection of free speech rights of all Americans, no matter how hateful their speech. Norman Siegel, executive director of the New York Civil Liberties Union, argues that censorship of any kind is the enemy of free speech. "The Internet should be an open, robust example of freedom of expression. The concept and the principle is that hate groups have First Amendment rights as they would have in an open marketplace of ideas. So if you can say X, Y, and Z on a street corner on a platform with a microphone, then the same principles and rules should apply on the Internet."

Other Forms of Hate Speech

Hate speech can show up in popular music, too. Infamous musician Eminem has come under fire repeatedly for making derogatory remarks about women and gays in his songs, and the profanity he uses to do so. Nevertheless, he is more popular than ever and many argue that his art is absolutely protected by the First Amendment

Symbols qualify as protected speech if they are worn or displayed in a public place, before a general audience—even if they are symbols associated with hate speech like swastikas or burning crosses. However, the First Amendment does not protect such symbols when they are used to desecrate private property, such as burning a cross on someone else's lawn or spray-painting a swastika on a synagogue. In 1992, in *R. A. V. v. City of St. Paul, Minnesota,* the U.S. Supreme Court struck down a St. Paul, Minnesota ordinance that prohibited cross burnings. The city felt that because white supremacist groups historically have used cross burnings to intimidate the targets of their wrath, symbols such as cross burnings should be banned. The Supreme Court stated that the city cannot prosecute someone for the content of his or her speech in such a case but that it could arrest the cross-burner for criminal trespass and harassment.

Hate Speech on Campus

The ACLU has noted a rise in verbal abuse directed against people of color, lesbians and gay men, and other groups in recent years. Several notable incidents involving hate speech have occurred on the campuses of

American colleges and universities. Alarmed by the behavior and anxious to respond to the problem, many schools have adopted speech codes that prohibit speech that offends any group of people, based on race, gender, sexual orientation, ethnicity, or religion.

For instance, in February 1991, Brown University expelled a student who had been found guilty of shouting racist, anti-Semitic, and homophobic statements outside a dormitory. The student was drunk at the time, as well. Brown University has rules against "showing flagrant disrespect for the well-being of others," taking part in "abusive, threatening or demeaning actions based on race, religion, gender, handicap, ethnicity, national origin, or sexual orientation," and drinking too much alcohol.

Certainly, it might seem like a good idea to remove someone like that from the school. The university was heavily criticized for violating the First Amendment, though. Critics argued that the university's expulsion of the student amounted to limiting free speech. The president of the school, Vartan Gregorian, wrote a letter to the *New York Times*, which was published that same month. He argued that Brown had not expelled the student for free speech. Gregorian explained that the school's code of conduct "does not prohibit speech; it prohibits actions, and these include behavior that 'shows flagrant disrespect for the well-being of others' . . . The rules do not proscribe [limit] words, epithets, or slanders; they proscribe behavior." President Gregorian went on to say that distinguishing between speech and behavior at Brown is determined on a case-by-case basis at a formal hearing.

Brown University students protest the running of an advertisement they consider to be hate speech in the student newspaper in March 2001.

At what point did the student's speech become behavior? This is the question asked by defenders of free speech. The ACLU defends a student's right to say those things, and opposes codes of conduct like that at Brown University for limiting speech. Critics of hate speech ordinances like the ACLU argue that colleges are, after all, not just places where students take classes, but centers dedicated to the exchange of ideas. Not all the ideas young people are exposed to at college are positive, nor will students agree with everything they hear. What if hate speech inhibits the educational experience of the students that it targets, such as women, racial minorities, and lesbians and gays?

Opposition to Hate Speech Policies

The ACLU has opposed any policies on college campuses that restrict speech. The ACLU has challenged university speech codes at the University of Connecticut, the University of Michigan, the University of Wisconsin, and the University of California. In 1990, the ACLU adopted a new policy on free speech and bias on college campuses. The ACLU believes that "all members of the academic community have the right to hold and to express views that others may find repugnant, offensive or emotionally distressing." The ACLU encourages colleges and universities to deal with bigotry through education and speech. It believes that freedom of thought and expression:

> is particularly important on the college campuses. The education forum is where individuals come together to participate in a process of shared inquiry and where the success of that endeavor depends on an atmosphere of openness, intellectual honesty, and tolerance for the ideas and opinions of others, even when hateful or offensive.

Stemming from the Enlightenment ideals that fueled the writing of the Constitution and the Bill of Rights, many lawmakers believe that laws always have been and should continue to apply universally, to everyone equally. Laws are neutral; laws should not attempt to redress past or current inequalities. Laws should not include or address categories of people; laws apply to all of the people all of the time. Unfortunately, what this line of reasoning tends to overlook is that the Constitution itself was written by a specific and legally exclusive group of people: propertied, (some slave-holding) white, Christian men.

Louis Farrakhan (1933–)

Farrakhan is one of the leaders of the Nation of Islam. Once he joined the Nation of Islam, Farrakhan quickly took on leadership positions. Farrakhan was a strong supporter of Jesse Jackson, particularly during his bid to become the Democratic Party's presidential nominee in the 1984 election. As he traveled the country, on Jackson's behalf, Farrakhan had made some controversial remarks.

During a radio speech, he called Adolf Hitler a great man, and soon found the press and the Anti-Defamation League (ADL) labeling him an anti-Semite. The ADL is a watchdog for organized bigotry. It collects information on anti-Semites, racists, and extremists of all kinds. After carefully evaluating information, the ADL disseminates that information through books, periodicals, videos, reports, and other materials. The League also monitors hate on the Web. Farrakhan still continues his work with the Nation of Islam, although he seems to be moving away from its racial beliefs and more toward the orthodox Islamic belief system.

Unintended Effects

Limiting free speech in an effort to silence those who will say aggressively hateful things can sometimes backfire. Two women, feminist activist and writer Andrea Dworkin and feminist legal scholar Catherine McKinnon, developed a plan to outlaw pornography. They claimed that pornography is a form of hate speech against women. Their argument was that pornography subordinates and demeans women in the eyes of the public, and that it consequently diminishes their social and economic status. For instance, if women are no more than sexual objects, some might argue, why employ them, or why pay them as much as you pay your male employees? Why treat them well at all?

Dworkin and McKinnon were not successful in the United States, but Canada did pass a censorship law. However, the first authors to be banned as a result were well-known gay writers, a radical black feminist, and even Andrea Dworkin herself. These people were obviously not the intended targets of the law but they used explicit language and referenced the female body in their work. Their conservative opponents used the law against them.

Some scholars argue that the reaction of targeted individuals to hate speech depends entirely on the individual. Some people will be frightened or intimidated; others will be inspired to take action. Some people will be silenced by hate speech, but there are others who respond by boldly voicing their views. Rather than force haters into silence, some argue that we should educate them. Their speeches should be met with opposing speeches. In 1927,

Speech That Is Not Protected

- Unwanted speech (words directed specifically at someone who does not want to hear them)
- Obscene speech
- Fighting words (words that will and are intended to start a fight)
- Personal threats
- Fraudulent speech
- Slander (spoken false statements that hurt others' reputations)
- Libel (printed false statements that hurt others)

Supreme Court Justice Louis Brandeis said, "If there be time to expose through discussion the falsehood and fallacies, to avert the evil by the processes of education, the remedy to be applied is more speech, not enforced silence." Like Brandeis, many Supreme Court justices have examined laws to see whether they are content-neutral, and ensure that a law does not favor an opinion or set of ideals at the expense of another.

Brandenburg v. Ohio (1969)

Hate speech was the focus of the case of Clarence Brandenburg, the leader of a Ku Klux Klan (KKK) group in Ohio. Brandenburg gave a speech at a KKK rally on the outskirts of Cincinnati. The event was filmed, and parts of the speech were shown on television. People who watched the broadcast saw twelve figures in white hoods, some holding shotguns. They were gathered around a burning cross, where they listened to Brandenburg. The leader's speech was full of hateful messages, including, "Send the Jews back to Israel," and "Freedom for whites."

Brandenburg was tried in an Ohio state court under a law that made it illegal to urge others to commit acts of violence and terrorism as a method of bringing about political change. The law also made it illegal to gather with others to teach or support the use of violence and force. Brandenburg was convicted, but he appealed to Ohio's Supreme Court and subsequently to the U.S. Supreme Court. The Supreme Court justices looked carefully at what Brandenburg had said: ". . . if our president, our Congress, our Supreme Court, continues to suppress the white, Caucasian race, it's possible that there might have to be some revengeance taken." The justices also looked at the law Brandenburg was accused of breaking.

A law that punishes advocacy, or actively supporting one's beliefs, the Supreme Court decided, is unconstitutional. Similarly, so is a law that does not allow assembly with others to advocate action. Such a law violates both the First and Fourteenth Amendments. Charles Brandenburg's conviction was overturned. A case that took place two decades earlier, similarly examined the issue of insulting or derisive speech and how that might advocate action.

Chaplinsky v. New Hampshire (1942)

On April 6, 1940, Walter Chaplinsky, a Jehovah's Witness, stood outside the city hall of Rochester, New Hampshire. There he passed out literature and announced to passersby that all religion is a racket. Angry citizens began to complain, so Rochester city marshall James Bowering warned Chaplinsky not to start a riot, threatening him with arrest. In response to this threat, Chaplinsky allegedly said, "You are a God-damned racketeer" and a "damned Fascist" and "the whole government of Rochester are Fascists." Bowering arrested Chaplinsky for breaking New Hampshire's fighting words law. The law reads as follows: "No person shall address any offensive, derisive or annoying word to any other person who is lawfully in any street or other public place, nor call him by any offensive or derisive name, nor make any noise or exclamation in his presence and hearing with intent to deride, offend or annoy him, or to prevent him from pursuing his lawful business or occupation."

Chaplinsky was found guilty and appealed the verdict, which was upheld by the New Hampshire Supreme Court. Chaplinsky argued that the fighting words statute limited freedom of speech, freedom of the press, and freedom of worship. He also claimed that the law was vague and indefinite. The case, on appeal again, finally went to the U.S. Supreme Court in 1942.

The Court turned its attention to the New Hampshire law, carefully discussing the limits of free speech:

> It is well understood that the right of free speech is not absolute at all times and under all circumstances. There are certain well-defined and narrowly limited classes of speech, the prevention and punishment of which have never been thought to raise any constitutional problem. These include the lewd and obscene, the profane, the libelous, and the insulting or 'fighting words'— those by which their very utterance inflict injury or tend to incite an immediate breach of the peace.

The purpose of the state's fighting words law was to keep the peace, with no words forbidden "except such as have a direct tendency to cause acts of violence by the persons to whom…the remark is addressed." To deal with the issues raised by the term "offensive," the law does not define it according to an individual's reaction, but by "what men of common intelligence would understand would be words likely to cause an average person to fight."

These criteria beg the question: What constitutes common intelligence? Who is the average person? Because the Court supported the notion that it is possible to define words clearly that would start an argument, they held that the New Hampshire statute was legal and that it did not violate Chaplinsky's right to free speech. Obviously, distinguishing between speech, action, and speech that inspires action can become quite difficult.

8 Free Speech and You

It may seem to you as though a lot of the Supreme Court cases examined in this book are removed from your own experiences, but this is simply not true. Take, for instance, Mary Beth Tinker's black armband—she paved the way for you to wear a red ribbon for AIDS awareness, a pink ribbon to support breast cancer research, a yellow ribbon to support people in the military, including those still missing in action. There are even ribbons to support free speech; many Web sites show a blue ribbon to support free speech online. Further, the Gobitas family fought for your right to refuse to salute the American flag, if you disagree with it, at your school. Some say, however that this right is not yet fully protected.

The Freedom Forum

The Freedom Forum, an organization devoted to protecting the rights of all Americans, has been tracking a movement to enforce the daily recital of the Pledge of Allegiance. In 1998, it reported the following events:

- A sixteen-year-old in Florida refused to stand and recite the pledge. He was angry at the way the government had treated his father, a Marine Corps veteran with cancer. He was suspended from the school for a day.

- In Seattle, Washington, a thirteen-year-old Jehovah's Witness refused to say the pledge for religious reasons, and his teacher sent him outside to stand in the rain for fifteen minutes.

- In San Diego, California, a sixteen-year-old girl refused to say the pledge because she didn't believe in God. The teacher tried to make her stand alone and recite it; when the girl still refused, the teacher gave her detention.

The rights of these students were clearly violated; in 1943 the Supreme Court ruled that forcing children to recite the pledge against their personal beliefs is to deny them their freedom.

Massie v. Henry (1972)

Does your school have rules about how you dress? Does it have rules about your hairstyle, too? In 1972, a case went before the United States Court of Appeals for the Second Circuit about just that—hair. Joseph Massie and a number of other male students were suspended from Tuscola High School in North Carolina. They had failed to obey a school guideline that regulated hair length and length of side-burns. The president of the student body asked for the passage of such a regulation in response to a specific incident.

A fight had occurred when one student had called another with long hair a hippie. Two other long-haired students reported that they had been threatened by other students. Teachers also complained. One said Massie and the others had trouble writing on the board in class because they had hair in their eyes, and a shop teacher claimed he would not let boys with long hair into his classroom for safety reasons.

Massie and the others wore their hair past their collars and covering their ears, and at least two of the boys had sideburns that extended below their ears. They objected to the school's attempt to regulate their personal appearance and took their case against the chairman of the board of education, Stanley Henry, to federal district court. The court said no constitutional rights had been violated and dismissed the case. On appeal, it went to the federal court of appeals, whereupon the decision was reversed. Circuit Judge Winter delivered the verdict:

> Whether the right of a male to wear long hair and to have long or fulsome sideburns is a constitutionally protected right is a question which has given birth to a rash of recent litigation . . . and if the right is recognized as a constitutionally protected one, there is a lack of agreement as to . . . the chapter and verse of the Constitution which protects it . . . Many

of the founding fathers, as well as General Grant and General Lee, wore their hair (either real or false) in a style comparable to that adopted by [Massie]. Although there exists no depiction of Jesus Christ, either reputedly or historically accurate, He has always been shown with hair at least the length of that of [Massie]. If the validity and enforcement of the regulation in issue is sustained, it follows that none of these persons would have been permitted to attend Tuscola Senior High School.

The judge also pointed out that there is some confusion about which part of the Constitution protects a person's right to wear his or her hair how he or she chooses. He also noted that such an issue is rather silly, as the way a person's hair looks is most often determined by the fashion of the time in which the person lives. He named historical figures that the court was likely to respect, pointing out that their long hair would have kept them out of school, too.

He went on to enumerate cases focusing on similar issues. In *Ferrell v. Dallas Independent School District* (1968), the court upheld the validity of a school rule forbidding a "Beatle-type haircut," and in *Jackson v. Dorrier (1970)*, the court held that there was no violation of the First Amendment when long hair was outlawed as a result of it having caused classroom disturbance. In other cases, he said, the right to have hair of whatever length a person chooses was shown to be a right of due process under both the First and Ninth Amendments. The Ninth Amendment protects rights given to us by the rest of the Constitution. Winter concluded:

> We see no inherent reason why decency, decorum, or good conduct requires a boy to wear his hair short. Certainly, eccentric hair styling is no longer a reliable sign of perverse behavior. We do not believe that mere unattractiveness in the eyes of some parents, teachers, or students, short of uncleanliness [there were no complaints against the boys about hygiene], can justify proscription. Nor, finally, does such compelled conformity to conventional standards of appearance seem a justifiable part of the educational process.

This last sentence of the court's verdict is particularly important. "Compelled conformity to conventional standards of appearance" is something that is an abomination to American principles of freedom and to the country's tradition of diversity. We cannot all look alike, nor should we. Who decides how we should look—the majority? Such a structure would deny millions of people their rights, because there are many aspects of our appearance that we really cannot change.

Winter also said, however, that "faculty leadership in promoting and enforcing an attitude of tolerance rather than one of suppression or derision would [prevent] the relatively minor disruptions which have occurred." In addition, he said that it would be fine for the school to require that students restrain their hair (tie it back) during classes such as shop, where their hair might pose a threat to their safety and the safety of others.

Banning Books

There are other ways in which your freedoms can be violated. Imagine you were in a bookstore and saw a couple of novels you really wanted to read, but only had enough money for one book. You decide to buy one and take the other out of the library. When you can't find the book on the school library shelves, you ask the librarian where you might find it, and he says, "That book is no longer available here because it contains some language and ideas that some people find offensive and that may affect your morals." This may sound improbable, but on the Internet, there are sites that list the top 100 books that are challenged each year by parent organizations, school boards, and other groups who want to dictate what you read. One such case went before the Supreme Court back in 1982.

Island Trees School Board v. Pico (1982)

In 1976, the Island Trees School Board of Long Island, New York, banned a number of books from their junior and senior high-school libraries. The titles were the anonymously written *Go Ask Alice*, Alice Childress' *A Hero Ain't Nothin' But a Sandwich*, Eldridge Cleaver's *Soul on Ice*, an anthology edited by Langston Hughes called *The Best Short Stories of Negro Writers*, Desmond Morris's *The Naked Ape*,

Piri Thomas's *Down These Mean Streets*, Kurt Vonnegut's *Slaughterhouse Five*, and Richard Wright's *Black Boy*. The school board said that its duty was to "protect the children in [their] schools from this moral danger as surely as from physical and medical dangers." In fact, they said it was their "moral obligation" to keep from children books they deemed to be "anti-American, anti-Christian, anti-Semitic, vulgar, immoral, and just plain filthy."

Steven Pico was an Island Trees student, and he (along with some other students) took the school board to court for violating his First Amendment right to read the speech of others. He demanded that the books be returned to the library. The U.S. District Court found for the school board. When the case went next to the court of appeals, Pico won. The board appealed, and the case went before the U.S. Supreme Court in 1982.

The Court addressed the essential issue of the case: Does the First Amendment limit a school board's right to remove books from junior and senior high-school libraries? Justice William Brennan, who delivered the opinion of the Court, first pointed out that the students were not looking to restrict the school board's power over curricula. They objected to the school board banning library books, books that are optional, rather than required, reading. In addition, Pico and the other students were only challenging the board's right to remove books placed there by school authorities; they were not demanding that the board add new books to the library. The Court agreed that "local school boards must be permitted 'to establish and apply their curriculum in such a way as to transmit community values,'" but it must do so with deference to the First Amendment.

Justice Brennan continued: "Our precedents have focused not only on the role of the First Amendment in fostering individual self-expression but also on its role in affording the public access to discussion, debate, and the dissemination of information and ideas." In other words, public schools are supposed to offer free access (within reason) to information and ideas. "The State may not, consistently with the spirit of the First Amendment, contract the spectrum of available knowledge . . . [And so] we have held that in a variety of contexts 'the Constitution protects the right to receive information and ideas.'"

Brennan went on to argue that an individual's right to receive ideas comes directly from another's right to communicate them; you can not have one without the other. As the Court found in *Tinker v. Des Moines*, "Students may not be regarded as close-circuit recipients of only that which the state chooses to communicate . . . School officials cannot suppress expressions of feeling with which they do not wish to contend."

The Court went on to describe the unique role of a school library as a place where "a student can literally explore the unknown." It is a place where students can expand on curriculum material and go beyond it; it is the place where they "remain free to inquire." Justice Brennan concluded that school boards can:

> determine the content of their school libraries. But that discretion may not be exercised in a narrowly partisan or political manner . . . Our Constitution

does not permit the official suppression of ideas. Thus whether [the board's] removal of books from their school libraries denied [the students] their First Amendment rights depends upon the motivation behind [the board's] actions. If [it] intended by its removal decision to deny [the students] access to ideas with which [it] disagreed, and if this intent was the decisive factor in [the] decision, then [it has] exercised [its] discretion in violation of the Constitution . . . Nothing in our decision today affects in any way the discretion of a local school board to choose books to add to the libraries . . . but we hold that local school boards may not remove books from school library shelves simply because they dislike the ideas contained in those books.

Steven Pico's case did not bring an end to efforts to restrict the free flow of ideas in this country. Today, many individuals and groups are still working to regulate your access to certain books, television and radio programs, movies, and works of art.

The Federal Communication Commission and the V-Chip

In response to the outcry that many television shows watched by children contain objectionable material, the federal government has been looking to technology for a method of blocking certain shows. Within the Federal

Communication Commission's (FCC) Telecommunications Act of 1996, Congress included a provision called "Parental Choice in Television Programming," commonly known as the V-Chip law. The law requires television networks to give their shows ratings that indicate the level of sexual content, violence, explicit language, or otherwise problematic content within the show, similar to the way in which movies are rated.

Currently, homes can be equipped with a device that allows parents to block reception of programs that are rated as overly sexual, violent, or problematic. This is a free speech concern, according to the Freedom Forum, because of "the process of devising and implementing a system called for in the law." In the bill itself, there was no mention of which shows were to be rated and who was going to do the rating. Critics of the V-Chip law assert that this legislation is a form of censorship, that it "amounts to an intrusion by the federal government into television programming." In 1997, in response to the V-Chip law, television industry executives proposed their own ratings system. Parents' organizations and others disliked these ratings because they felt that they were not sufficiently narrow.

Proponents of the V-Chip law maintain that it was merely intended to help parents control what their children watch. It can still be seen as an effort on the part of the government to control media content, and so First Amendment watchdogs are on the alert. Television is not the only medium the government has tried to restrict. The newest communications frontier—the Internet—is the subject of much debate regarding free speech rights.

RATING WHAT YOU WATCH

TVY and TVK: suitable for all children

TVY7: designated for children age seven and over

TV-G: suitable for entire audience; parents may leave children unattended

TV-PG: parental guidance suggested as program may contain material that some parents may find unsuitable for younger children

TV-14: parents strongly cautioned as program may contain infrequent coarse language, limited violence, some suggestive sexual dialogue and situations

TV-M: designed for mature audiences and may contain profane language, graphic violence, and explicit sexual content

Regulating the Internet

In response to some highly publicized cases of children being exposed to pornographic material online, lawmakers began to argue for laws that would regulate content on the Internet. The Communications Decency Act (CDA) was enacted by Congress as part of the Telecommunications Decency Act of 1996. The CDA did three things: It made illegal the transmission of "any comment, request, suggestion, proposal, image, or other communication which is obscene, lewd lascivious, filthy or indecent, with intent to annoy, abuse, threaten, or harass another person." It also made it illegal to do so if the person transmitting knows the receiver to be under eighteen. Any expression that shows or describes sexual or excretory activities or organs and is available to anyone under eighteen was a criminal act, as well. The Web pages, newsgroups, chat rooms, and online discussion lists that would have been unavailable in the public forum included popular works of fiction such as J. D. Salinger's *The Catcher in the Rye*.

In 1997, the Supreme Court struck down the CDA in *Reno, Attorney General of the United States v. American Civil Liberties Union*. Justice John Paul Stevens wrote that "the CDA places an unacceptably heavy burden on protected speech" and found that each of the three parts of the CDA was unconstitutional as they apply to "indecent" or "patently offensive" speech, except for where narrowly applied to speech "between an adult and one or more minors." The Court ruled that the Internet is unique and entitled to the highest protection under the First Amendment. This gives information and ideas shared on the Internet the same protections that apply to printed material.

Conclusion

Free speech is not just about saying what you want. It is also about hearing what you want to hear, reading books you would like to read, listening to (or choosing to ignore) opinions with which you disagree, and accepting or rejecting meaning from a variety of symbols. We were given this important freedom so that we might keep ourselves safe from the tyranny of a government with too much power, and so that no one voice would have authority over all other voices.

Since the First Amendment was written, the country has undergone an awesome number of changes. The way we now communicate with each other is faster and more complex. As we have changed, so has the Constitution. Legislators, the courts, and many concerned citizens have seen to it that these rights adapt to suit changing circumstances. It is important not only that we exercise this right, speaking out for what we believe, but that we also protect this right for others.

Preamble to the Constitution

We the people of the United States, in order to form a more perfect Union, establish Justice, insure domestic Tranquility, provide for the common defence, promote the general Welfare, and secure the Blessings of Liberty to ourselves and our Posterity, do ordain and establish this Constitution for the United States of America

On September 25, 1789, Congress transmitted to the state legislatures twelve proposed amendments, two of which, having to do with congressional representation and congressional pay, were not adopted. The remaining ten amendments became the Bill of Rights.

The Bill of Rights

Amendment I

Congress shall make no law respecting an establishment of religion, or prohibiting the free exercise thereof; or abridging the freedom of speech, or of the press; or the right of the people peaceably to assemble, and to petition the Government for a redress of grievances.

Amendment II

A well regulated Militia, being necessary to the security of a free State, the right of the people to keep and bear Arms, shall not be infringed.

Amendment III

No Soldier shall, in time of peace be quartered in any house, without the consent of the Owner, nor in time of war, but in a manner to be prescribed by law.

Amendment IV

The right of the people to be secure in their persons, houses, papers, and effects, against unreasonable searches and seizures, shall not be violated, and no Warrants shall issue, but upon probable cause, supported by Oath or affirmation, and particularly describing the place to be searched, and the persons or things to be seized.

Amendment V

No person shall be held to answer for a capital, or otherwise infamous crime, unless on a presentment or indictment of a Grand Jury, except in cases arising in the land or naval forces, or in the Militia, when in actual service in time of War or public danger; nor shall any person be subject for the same offence to be twice put in jeopardy of life or limb; nor shall be compelled in any criminal case to be a witness against himself, nor be deprived of life, liberty, or property, without due process of law; nor shall private property be taken for public use, without just compensation.

Amendment VI

In all criminal prosecutions, the accused shall enjoy the right to a speedy and public trial, by an impartial jury of the State and district wherein the crime shall have been committed, which district shall have been previously ascertained by law, and to be informed of the nature and cause of the accusation; to be confronted with the witnesses against him; to have compulsory process for obtaining witnesses in his favor, and to have the Assistance of Counsel for his defence.

Amendment VII

In Suits at common law, where the value in controversy shall exceed twenty dollars, the right of trial by jury shall be preserved, and no fact tried by a jury, shall be otherwise re-examined in any Court of the United States, than according to the rules of the common law.

Amendment VIII

Excessive bail shall not be required, nor excessive fines imposed, nor cruel and unusual punishments inflicted.

Amendment IX

The enumeration in the Constitution, of certain rights, shall not be construed to deny or disparage others retained by the people.

Amendment X

The powers not delegated to the United States by the Constitution, nor prohibited by it to the States, are reserved to the States respectively, or to the people.

Glossary

anarchist A person who supports the idea that no one should be in control and that there should be no government.

boycott To refuse to buy something or take part in something as a way to protest.

civil rights The rights that all members of a society have to freedom and equal treatment under the law.

Communist A person who supports the idea that all land, property and goods, and businesses in a country belong to the government or the community, and everyone shares the profits.

Congress The branch of the U.S. government that makes laws. It is made up of the Senate and the House of Representatives.

conservative Someone who opposes radical change and wants things to stay as they are or as they used to be.

constitution A document that establishes the fundamental laws of a state or a country.

Continental Congress The first organized government in America outside of British rule.

dissent Disagreement with an opinion or an idea.

fighting words Any words directed at a specific person that would start a fight and endanger others.

inalienable Incapable of being surrendered.

legislation Laws that have been proposed or passed.

liberal Someone who is in favor of political change and reform.

monopoly Complete control of something, such as a supply of a product.

obscenity A word or image that is shocking and indecent.

pacifist A person who believes that war and violence are wrong and refuses to fight.

segregation The practice of keeping people of different races apart.

Socialist A person who supports an economic system in which the government controls the production of goods by factories, businesses, and farms.

subjects People who live under the authority of a king or queen.

Supreme Court Highest and most powerful court in the United States. It can declare laws unconstitutional.

For More Information

American Civil Liberties Union (ACLU)
125 Broad Street, 17th floor
New York, NY 10004
(212) 344-3005
Web site: http://www.aclu.org

Americans United for Separation of Church and State
518 C Street NE
Washington, DC 20002
(202) 466-3234
e-mail: americansunited@au.org
Web site: http://www.au.org

The Center for Democracy and Technology
1634 Eye Street NW, Suite 1100
Washington, DC 20006
(202)637-9800
e-mail: feedback@cdt.org
Web site: http://www.cdt.org

First Amendment Cyber-Tribune (FACT)
http://w3.trib.com/FACT

The Freedom Forum
First Amendment Center/New York
580 Madison Avenue
New York, NY 10022
212/317-6500
e-mail: info@fac.org
Web site: http://www.freedomforum.org

Freedom to Read Foundation
American Library Association
50 East Huron Street
Chicago, IL 60611
(800) 545-2433 ext. 4226
e-mail: ftrf@ala.org
Web site: http://www.ftrf.org

National Coalition Against Censorship (NCAC)
275 Seventh Avenue
New York, NY 10001
(212) 807-6222
Web site: http://www.ncac.org

OneWorld U.S.
Benton Foundation
1800 K Street NW, 2nd Floor
Washington, DC 20016
(202) 638-5770
Web site: http://www.oneworld.net/us/

People for the American Way
2000 M Street NE
Washington, DC 20036
(800) 326-PFAW (7329)
e-mail: pfaw@pfaw.org
Web site: http://www.pfaw.org

Student Press Law Center
1815 N. Fort Myer Drive, Suite 900
Arlington, VA 22209
(703) 807-1904
e-mail: splc@splc.org
Web site: http://www.splc.org

For Further Reading

Alonso, Karen. *Schenck V. United States: Restrictions on Free Speech.* Springfield, NJ: Enslow Publishers, Inc., 1999.

Farish, Leah. *The First Amendment: Freedom of Speech, Religion, and the Press.* Springfield, NJ: Enslow Publishers, Inc., 1998.

Farish, Leah. *Tinker V. Des Moines: Student Protest.* Springfield, NJ: Enslow Publishers, Inc., 1997.

Steele, Philip. *Freedom of Speech.* New York: Franklin Watts, 1997.

Steins, Richard. *Censorship: How Does It Conflict with Freedom?* New York: Twenty-first Century Books, 1995.

Trespacz, Karen. *Ferrell V. Dallas I.S.D: Hairstyles in Schools.* Springfield, NJ: Enslow Publishers, Inc., 1998.

Zeinert, Karen. *Free Speech: From Newspapers to Music Lyrics.* Springfield, NJ: Enslow Publishers, Inc., 1995.

Index

About the Author

Claudia Isler is a freelance editor and writer who has edited material ranging in subject from robotic engineering to soap operas. She has written other Rosen books for young people, including *Caught in the Middle: A Teen Guide to Custody* and *The Right to Vote*. She lives in Pennsylvania with her husband and their cat.

Photo Credits

Cover image: the Constitution of the United States of America; pp. 6, 7, 22 © Indexstock; pp. 17, 23 © Corbis; pp. 19, 26, 27, 31, 33, 34, 37, 39, 47, 49, 59, 89, 95, 97 © Associated Press AP; p. 53 © Archive Photos.